A DOLL'S
HOUSE

A DOLL'S HOUSE

HENRIK IBSEN

ARCTURUS

Picture credits: page 10: corbis; page 57: 'By Lamplight', 1890, by Harriet Backer (Ramus Meyers Samlinger, Bergen, Norway/The Bridgeman Art Library); page 94: Vera Komissarzhevskaya as Nora (akg images). Cover image based on "Empire of Light" by René Magritte.

ARCTURUS

This edition published in 2010 by Arcturus Publishing Limited
26/27 Bickels Yard, 151–153 Bermondsey Street,
London SE1 3HA

Copyright © 2010 Arcturus Publishing Limited

ISBN: 978-1-84837-591-8
AD001391EN

Printed in China

CONTENTS

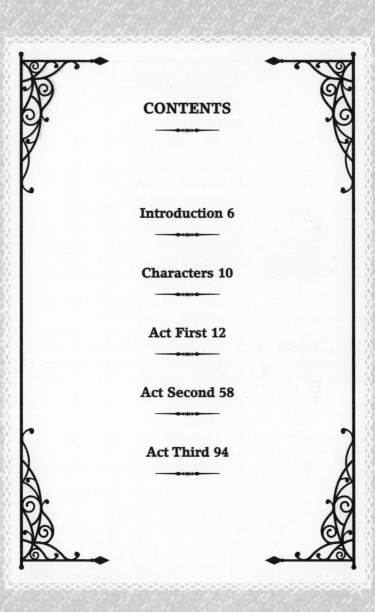

INTRODUCTION

> *There are two kinds of moral law, two kinds of*
> *conscience, one in men and a quite different one*
> *in women. They do not understand each other; but in*
> *matters of practical living a woman is judged by the*
> *men's law, as if she were not a woman but a man. ... ...*
> *A woman cannot be herself in present-day society, which*
> *is an exclusively male society with laws written by men,*
> *and with prosecutors and judges who judge female*
> *behaviour from the male point of view.*

So begin Henrik Ibsen's *Notes for the Contemporary Tragedy*, preliminary notes for what was to become one of his best-known plays, *Et Dukkehjem* "A Doll's House". These are, however, not the mere philosophical musings of a critical observer of European society: Ibsen is well aware of the consequences of the state of affairs he describes, and his notes continue:

> *She has committed a crime, and she is proud of it,*
> *because she did it out of love for her husband, to save*
> *his life. But the man, with his conventional views of*
> *honour, stands on the side of the law and looks at the*
> *matter through male eyes.*

Ibsen himself knew a young Norwegian woman, a writer, Laura Kieler, who had found herself in this very position. Laura's husband Victor had developed tuberculosis, and his doctor advised that he spend some time in a warmer climate. The couple being by no means well off, Laura secretly borrowed money to finance their trip to Switzerland and Italy, but finding herself in difficulty with her creditors, she resorted to forgery in order to pay her debts. Her crime was discovered, and regardless of the fact that it was only for love of him that she had committed it, her husband refused to stand by her, telling her she was not fit to look after their children and demanding a divorce. The mental distress this caused led to Laura being committed to a mental hospital. Soon discharged, she was eventually and somewhat grudgingly taken back by her husband, for the sake of their children.

Laura Kieler's story appears to have affected Ibsen deeply. Before desperation led her to have recourse to forgery, Laura had already unburdened herself to Ibsen's wife Suzannah. Early in 1878, informed of her plight, Ibsen had advised Laura to confide in her husband. And when in October of that same year Ibsen began work on *A Doll's House,* he was certainly already aware of how that real-life drama had played out; indeed, even as early as May he had mentioned to Frederik Hegel, his publisher in Copenhagen, that he was planning this new "drama of modern life". Although both the circumstances and the fate of Ibsen's heroine Nora Helmer differ in many respects from Laura's, the parallels between Laura and Victor Kieler and Nora and Torvald Helmer are obvious to anyone who reads Ibsen's play. Even Ibsen's advice to Laura that "whatever is troubling you, put everything in your husband's hands" is paralleled in the words of Mrs Linden that "Helmer must know everything; there must be an end to this unhappy secret". Mrs Linden expects, as Ibsen had expected, that with an end to "all these shifts and subterfuges" the couple will "come to a full understanding". She is wrong, as Ibsen had been. But in the end Nora, unlike Laura, takes control over the consequences of her own and her husband's actions, as she at last sees her husband and her marriage for what they are.

A Doll's House was published in Copenhagen in December 1879. The first printing of 8,000 copies was the largest edition of

any of Ibsen's works up to that time. Hugely successful, it sold
out in less than a month. A second printing of 4,000 copies
came out in January 1880, with a third printing of 2,500 copies
two months later. It went on to become an international success,
the first of Ibsen's works to enter the realms of world literature.
Less than three weeks after publication, the play premiered at the
Royal Theatre in Copenhagen. It was first performed in London
and New York in 1889 (although versions of the play had
already been produced in both England and the United States
during the 1880s).

The shock waves that the play created are perhaps hard to
understand today. Ibsen's biographer, Halvdan Koht, has said that
A Doll's House 'exploded like a bomb into contemporary life'.
Given the level of hostility that the play aroused – Ibsen even had
to rewrite the ending of the German version to make it more
acceptable – it is perhaps going too far to say, as Koht did, that it
"pronounced a death sentence on accepted social ethics", but
nevertheless, when Torvald tells Nora that "before all else you are
a wife and a mother" and that her "holiest duties" are to her
husband and her children, Nora's rejoinder that she has "other
duties equally sacred... duties towards myself" could certainly be
seen – and was seen – as an attack on, and a threat to,
contemporary understanding of a woman's role as wife and
mother within a marriage. Ibsen was even described as "an
obscene defiler of the purity of the home".

Although A Doll's House challenged the then accepted views
on the place of women in society and has since its earliest
performances been of immense significance in the struggle for equal
rights for women the world over, it must be stressed that it was not
in Ibsen's mind a play specifically about the rights of women. As
he said in a speech to the Norwegian Society for Women's Rights:
"I must disclaim the honour of having consciously worked for
women's rights. ... To me it has been a question of human rights."
As she closes the door on her doll's-house marriage, Nora herself

asserts that "before all else I am a human being". It is not only women who can relate to such an assertion.

Henrik Ibsen was born in 1828 and died in 1906. Hailed as the father of modern drama and credited with being the first major tragedian to write in prose about ordinary people in everyday situations, he has long been recognized not only as Norway's greatest dramatist (he was also a poet and an artist), but also as one of the world's great playwrights, second only to Shakespeare in popularity and in the number of performances of his plays. (In 2006, there were more than 8,000 celebratory events in over 80 countries to mark the hundredth anniversary of his death.) Ibsen's greatest works were not, however, written in his native country: he left Norway in 1864, and spent the next 27 years in Italy and Germany. *A Doll's House* was written in Rome and Amalfi. In 1891 Ibsen returned to Norway and settled in Christiania – the name given to the city of Oslo between 1624 and 1924 – where he lived until his death.

An early champion of Ibsen's work in Britain was the theatre critic William Archer (1856–1924). Born in Scotland but the grandson of a Scottish timber merchant who had settled in Norway, he translated several of Ibsen's works into English. It was his translation of *A Doll's House* that was performed in London in 1889 and that is reproduced here.

George Davidson

CHARACTERS

TORVALD HELMER

NORA, his wife

DOCTOR RANK

Mrs LINDEN*

NILS KROGSTAD

THE HELMERS' THREE CHILDREN

ANNA**, their nurse

A MAID-SERVANT (ELLEN)

A PORTER

The action passes in Helmer's house (a flat)

in Christiania.

*In the original "Fru Linde"
**In the original "Anne-Marie"

ACT FIRST

A room, comfortably and tastefully, but not expensively, furnished. In the back, on the right, a door leads to the hall; on the left another door leads to HELMER's study. Between the two doors a pianoforte. In the middle of the left wall a door, and nearer the front a window. Near the window a round table with armchairs and a small sofa. In the right wall, somewhat to the back, a door, and against the same wall, further forward, a porcelain stove; in front of it a couple of armchairs and a rocking chair. Between the stove and the side door a small table. Engravings on the walls. A what-not with china and bric-a-brac. A small bookcase filled with handsomely bound books. Carpet. A fire in the stove. It is a winter day.

A bell rings in the hall outside. Presently the outer door of the flat is heard to open. Then NORA enters, humming gaily. She is in outdoor dress, and carries several parcels, which she lays on the right-hand table. She leaves the door into the hall open, and a PORTER is seen outside, carrying a Christmas tree and a basket, which he gives to the MAID-SERVANT who has opened the door.

NORA Hide the Christmas tree carefully, Ellen; the children must on no account see it before this evening, when it's lighted up. [*To the PORTER, taking out her purse.*] How much?

PORTER Fifty öre*.

* *About sixpence. There are 100 öre in a krone or crown, which is worth thirteenpence halfpenny.*

NORA There is a crown. No, keep the change.

[*The PORTER thanks her and goes. NORA shuts the door. She continues smiling in quiet glee as she takes off her outdoor things. Taking from her pocket a bag of macaroons, she eats one or two. Then she goes on tip toe to her husband's door and listens.*]

NORA Yes, he is at home. [*She begins humming again, crossing to the table on the right.*]

HELMER [*In his room.*] Is that my lark twittering there?

NORA [*Busy opening some of her parcels.*] Yes, it is.

HELMER Is it the squirrel frisking around?

NORA Yes!

HELMER When did the squirrel get home?

NORA Just this minute. [*Hides the bag of macaroons in her pocket and wipes her mouth.*] Come here, Torvald, and see what I've been buying.

HELMER Don't interrupt me. [*A little later he opens the door and looks in, pen in hand.*] "Bought" did you say? What! All that? Has my little spendthrift been making the money fly again?

NORA Why, Torvald, surely we can afford to launch out a little now. It's the first Christmas we haven't had to pinch.

HELMER Come come; we can't afford to squander money.

NORA Oh yes, Torvald, do let us squander a little, now … just the least little bit! You know you'll soon be earning heaps of money.

HELMER Yes, from New Year's Day. But there's a whole quarter before my first salary is due.

NORA Never mind; we can borrow in the meantime.

HELMER Nora! [*He goes up to her and takes her playfully by the ear.*] Still my little featherbrain! Supposing I borrowed a thousand crowns today, and you made ducks and drakes of them during Christmas week, and then on New Year's Eve a tile blew off the roof and knocked my brains out...

NORA [*Laying her hand on his mouth.*] Hush! How can you talk so horridly?

HELMER But supposing it were to happen... what then?

NORA If anything so dreadful happened, it would be all the same to me whether I was in debt or not.

HELMER But what about the creditors?

NORA They! Who cares for them? They're only strangers.

HELMER Nora, Nora! What a woman you are! But seriously, Nora, you know my principles on these points. No debts! No borrowing! Home life ceases to be free and beautiful as soon as it is founded on borrowing and debt. We two have held out bravely till now, and we are not going to give in at the last.

NORA [*Going to the fireplace.*] Very well... as you please, Torvald.

HELMER [*Following her.*] Come come; my little lark mustn't droop her wings like that. What? Is my squirrel in the sulks? [*Takes out his purse.*] Nora, what do you think I have here?

NORA [*Turning round quickly.*] Money!

HELMER There! [*Gives her some notes.*] Of course, I know all sorts of things are wanted at Christmas.

NORA [*Counting.*] Ten, twenty, thirty, forty. Oh, thank you, thank you, Torvald! This will go a long way.

HELMER I should hope so.

NORA Yes, indeed; a long way! But come here, and let me show you all I've been buying. And so cheap! Look, here's a new suit for Ivar, and a little sword. Here are a horse and a trumpet for Bob. And here are a doll and a cradle for Emmy. They're only common; but they're good enough for her to pull to pieces. And dress stuffs and kerchiefs for the servants. I ought to have got something better for old Anna.

HELMER And what's in that other parcel?

NORA [*Crying out.*] No, Torvald, you're not to see that until this evening.

HELMER Oh! Ah! But now tell me, you little spendthrift, have you thought of anything for yourself?

NORA For myself! Oh, I don't want anything.

HELMER Nonsense! Just tell me something sensible you would like to have.

NORA No, really I don't know of anything... Well, listen, Torvald...

HELMER Well?

NORA [*Playing with his coat buttons, without looking him in the face.*] If you really want to give me something, you might, you know... you might...

HELMER Well? Out with it!

NORA [*Quickly.*] You might give me money, Torvald. Only just what you think you can spare; then I can buy something with it later on.

HELMER But, Nora...

NORA Oh, please do, dear Torvald, please do! I should hang the money in lovely gilt paper on the Christmas tree. Wouldn't that be fun?

HELMER What do they call the birds that are always making the money fly?

NORA Yes, I know... spendthrifts*, of course. But please do as I ask you, Torvald. Then I shall have time to think what I want most. Isn't that very sensible, now?

HELMER [*Smiling.*] Certainly; that is to say, if you really kept the money I gave you, and really spent it on something for yourself. But it all goes in housekeeping, and for all manner of useless things, and then I have to pay up again.

NORA But, Torvald...

HELMER Can you deny it, Nora dear? [*He puts his arm round her.*] It's a sweet little lark, but it gets through a lot of money. No one would believe how much it costs a man to keep such a little bird as you.

* *"Spillefugl", literally "playbird", means a gambler.*

NORA For shame! How can you say so? Why, I save as much as ever I can.

HELMER [*Laughing.*] Very true... as much as you can... but that's precisely nothing.

NORA [*Hums and smiles in quiet satisfaction.*] Hm! If you only knew, Torvald, what expenses we larks and squirrels have.

HELMER You're a strange little being! Just like your father... always on the look-out for all the money you can lay your hands on; but the moment you have it, it seems to slip through your fingers; you never know what becomes of it. Well, one must take you as you are. It's in the blood. Yes, Nora, that sort of thing is inherited.

NORA I wish I had inherited many of papa's qualities.

HELMER And I don't wish you anything but just what you are... my own, sweet little song bird. But I say... it strikes me you look so, so... what shall I call it?... so suspicious today...

NORA Do I?

HELMER You do, indeed. Look me full in the face.

NORA [*Looking at him.*] Well?

HELMER [*Threatening with his finger.*] Hasn't the little sweet-tooth been playing pranks today?

NORA No; how can you think such a thing!

HELMER Didn't she just look in at the confectioner's?

NORA No, Torvald; really...

HELMER Not to sip a little jelly?

NORA No; certainly not.

HELMER Hasn't she even nibbled a macaroon or two?

NORA No, Torvald, indeed, indeed!

HELMER Well, well, well; of course, I'm only joking.

NORA [*Goes to the table on the right.*] I shouldn't think of doing what you disapprove of.

HELMER No, I'm sure of that; and, besides, you've given me your word… [*Going towards her.*] Well, keep your little Christmas secrets to yourself, Nora darling. The Christmas tree will bring them all to light, I dare say.

NORA Have you remembered to invite Doctor Rank?

HELMER No. But it's not necessary; he'll come as a matter of course. Besides, I shall ask him when he looks in today. I've ordered some capital wine. Nora, you can't think how I look forward to this evening.

NORA And I too. How the children will enjoy themselves, Torvald!

HELMER Ah, it's glorious to feel that one has an assured position and ample means. Isn't it delightful to think of?

NORA Oh, it's wonderful!

HELMER Do you remember last Christmas? For three whole weeks beforehand you shut yourself up every evening till long past midnight to make flowers for the Christmas tree, and all sorts of other marvels that were to have astonished us. I was never so bored in my life.

NORA I didn't bore myself at all.

HELMER [*Smiling.*] But it came to little enough in the end, Nora.

NORA Oh, are you going to tease me about that again? How could I help the cat getting in and pulling it all to pieces?

HELMER To be sure you couldn't, my poor little Nora. You did your best to give us all pleasure, and that's the main point. But, all the same, it's a good thing the hard times are over.

NORA Oh, isn't it wonderful?

HELMER Now I needn't sit here boring myself all alone; and you needn't tire your blessed eyes and your delicate little fingers…

NORA [*Clapping her hands.*] No, I needn't, need I, Torvald? Oh, how wonderful it is to think of. [*Takes his arm.*] And now I'll tell you how I think we ought to manage, Torvald. As soon as Christmas is over… [*The hall door bell rings.*] Oh, there's a ring! [*Arranging the room.*] That's somebody come to call. How tiresome!

HELMER I'm "not at home" to callers; remember that.

ELLEN [*In the doorway.*] A lady to see you, ma'am.

NORA Show her in.

ELLEN [*To HELMER.*] And the doctor has just come, sir.

HELMER Has he gone into my study?

ELLEN Yes, sir.

[*HELMER goes into his study. ELLEN ushers in Mrs LINDEN, in travelling costume, and goes out, closing the door behind her.*]

MRS LINDEN [*Timidly and hesitantly.*] How do you do, Nora?

NORA [*Doubtfully.*] How do you do?

MRS LINDEN I daresay you don't recognise me!

NORA No, I don't think... oh yes!... I believe... [*Suddenly effusive.*] What, Christina! Is it really you?

MRS LINDEN Yes; really I!

NORA Christina! And to think I didn't know you! But how could I... [*More softly.*] How changed you are, Christina!

MRS LINDEN Yes, no doubt. In nine or ten years...

NORA Is it really so long since we met? Yes, so it is. Oh, the last eight years have been a happy time, I can tell you. And now you have come to town? All that long journey in midwinter! How brave of you!

MRS LINDEN I arrived by this morning's steamer.

NORA To have a merry Christmas, of course. Oh, how delightful! Yes, we will have a merry Christmas. Do take your things off. Aren't you frozen? [*Helping her.*] There; now we'll sit cosily by the fire. No, you take the armchair; I shall sit in this rocking chair. [*Seizes her hands.*] Yes, now I can see the dear old face again. It was only at the first glance... But you're a little paler, Christina... and perhaps a little thinner.

Mrs LINDEN And much, much older, Nora.

NORA Yes, perhaps a little older... not much... ever so little. [*She suddenly stops; seriously.*] Oh, what a thoughtless wretch I am! Here I sit chattering on, and... Dear, dear Christina, can you forgive me!

Mrs LINDEN What do you mean, Nora?

NORA [*Softly.*] Poor Christina! I forgot: you are a widow.

Mrs LINDEN Yes; my husband died three years ago.

NORA I know, I know; I saw it in the papers. Oh, believe me, Christina, I did mean to write to you; but I kept putting it off, and something always came in the way.

Mrs LINDEN I can quite understand that, Nora dear.

NORA No, Christina; it was horrid of me. Oh, you poor darling! How much you must have gone through!... And he left you nothing?

Mrs LINDEN Nothing.

NORA And no children?

Mrs LINDEN None.

NORA Nothing, nothing at all?

Mrs LINDEN Not even a sorrow or a longing to dwell upon.

NORA [*Looking at her incredulously.*] My dear Christina, how is that possible?

MRS LINDEN [*Smiling sadly and stroking her hair.*] Oh, it happens so sometimes, Nora.

NORA So utterly alone! How dreadful that must be! I have three of the loveliest children. I can't show them to you just now; they're out with their nurse. But now you must tell me everything.

MRS LINDEN No, no; I want you to tell me...

NORA No, you must begin; I won't be egotistical today. Today I'll think only of you. Oh! but I must tell you one thing... perhaps you've heard of our great stroke of fortune?

MRS LINDEN No. What is it?

NORA Only think! My husband has been made manager of the Joint Stock Bank.

MRS LINDEN Your husband! Oh, how fortunate!

NORA Yes; isn't it? A lawyer's position is so uncertain, you see, especially when he won't touch any business that's the least bit shady, as of course Torvald never would; and there I quite agree with him. Oh! You can imagine how glad we are. He is to enter on his new position at the New Year, and then he'll have a large salary, and percentages. In future we shall be able to live quite differently... just as we please, in fact. Oh, Christina, I feel so lighthearted and happy! It's delightful to have lots of money, and no need to worry about things, isn't it?

MRS LINDEN Yes; at any rate it must be delightful to have what you need.

NORA No, not only what you need, but heaps of money... heaps!

MRS LINDEN [*Smiling.*] Nora, Nora, haven't you learnt reason yet? In our school days you were a shocking little spendthrift.

NORA [*Quietly smiling.*] Yes; that's what Torvald says I am still. [*Shaking her forefinger.*] But "Nora, Nora" is not so silly as you all think. Oh! I haven't had the chance to be much of a spendthrift. We have both had to work.

MRS LINDEN You too?

NORA Yes, light fancy work: crochet and embroidery, and things of that sort; [*significantly*] and other work too. You know, of course, that Torvald left the Government service when we were married. He had little chance of promotion, and of course, he required to make more money. But in the first year after our marriage he overworked himself terribly. He had to undertake all sorts of extra work, you know, and to slave early and late. He couldn't stand it, and fell dangerously ill. Then the doctors declared he must go to the South.

MRS LINDEN Yes, you spent a whole year in Italy, didn't you?

NORA Yes, we did. It wasn't easy to manage, I can tell you. It was just after Ivar's birth. But of course we had to go. Oh, it was a delicious journey! And it saved Torvald's life. But it cost a frightful lot of money, Christina.

MRS LINDEN So I should think.

NORA Twelve hundred dollars! Four thousand eight hundred crowns!* Isn't that a lot of money?

* The dollar (4s. 6d.) was the old unit of currency in Norway. The crown was substituted for it shortly before the date of this play.

MRS LINDEN How lucky you had the money to spend!

NORA We got it from father, you must know.

MRS LINDEN Ah, I see. He died just about that time, didn't he?

NORA Yes, Christina, just then. And only think! I couldn't go and nurse him! I was expecting little Ivar's birth daily; and then I had my poor sick Torvald to attend to. Dear, kind old father! I never saw him again, Christina. Oh! that's the hardest thing I have had to bear since my marriage.

MRS LINDEN I know how fond you were of him. But then you went to Italy?

NORA Yes, we had the money, and the doctors said we must lose no time. We started a month later.

MRS LINDEN And your husband returned completely cured.

NORA Sound as a bell.

MRS LINDEN But... the doctor?

NORA What do you mean?

MRS LINDEN I thought as I came in your servant announced the doctor...

NORA Oh, yes; Doctor Rank. But he doesn't come professionally. He is our best friend, and never lets a day pass without looking in. No, Torvald hasn't had an hour's illness since that time. And the children are so healthy and well, and so am I. [*Jumps up and claps her hands.*] Oh, Christina, Christina, what a wonderful thing it is to live and to be happy!... Oh, but it's really too horrid of me! Here am I talking about nothing but my own concerns. [*Seats herself upon a footstool close to her, and lays her arms on* CHRISTINA's *lap.*] Oh! Don't be angry with me! Now tell me, is it really true that you didn't love your husband? What made you marry him, then?

MRS LINDEN My mother was still alive, you see, bedridden and helpless; and then I had my two younger brothers to think of. I thought it my duty to accept him.

NORA Perhaps it was. I suppose he was rich then?

MRS LINDEN Very well off, I believe. But his business was uncertain. It fell to pieces at his death, and there was nothing left.

NORA And then…?

MRS LINDEN Then I had to fight my way by keeping a shop, a little school, anything I could turn my hand to. The last three years have been one long struggle for me. But now it is over, Nora. My poor mother no longer needs me; she is at rest. And the boys are in business, and can look after themselves.

NORA How free your life must feel!

MRS LINDEN No, Nora, only inexpressibly empty. No one to live for! [*Stands up restlessly.*] That's why I could not bear to stay any longer in that out-of-the-way corner. Here it must be easier to find something to take one up… to occupy one's thoughts. If I could only get some settled employment… some office work.

NORA But, Christina, that's such drudgery, and you look worn out already. You should rather go to some watering place and rest.

MRS LINDEN [*Going to the window.*] I have no father to give me the money, Nora.

NORA [*Rising.*] Oh, don't be vexed with me.

Mrs LINDEN [*Going to her.*] My dear Nora, don't you be vexed with me. The worst of a position like mine is that it makes one so bitter. You have no one to work for, yet you have to be always on the strain. You must live; and so you become selfish. When I heard of the happy change in your fortunes... can you believe it?... I was glad for my own sake more than for yours.

NORA How do you mean? Ah, I see! You think Torvald can perhaps do something for you.

Mrs LINDEN Yes; I thought so.

NORA And so he shall, Christina. Just you leave it all to me. I shall lead up to it beautifully!... I shall think of some delightful plan to put him in a good humour! Oh, I should so love to help you.

Mrs LINDEN How good of you, Nora, to stand by me so warmly! Doubly good in you, who knows so little of the troubles and burdens of life.

NORA I? I know so little of...?

Mrs LINDEN [*Smiling.*] Oh, well... a little fancy-work, and so forth. You're a mere child, Nora.

NORA [*Tosses her head and paces the room.*] Oh, come, you mustn't be so patronising!

Mrs LINDEN No?

NORA You're like the rest. You all think I'm fit for nothing really serious...

MRS LINDEN Well...

NORA You think I've had no troubles in this weary world.

MRS LINDEN My dear Nora, you've just told me all your troubles.

NORA Pooh... those trifles! [*Softly.*] I haven't told you the great thing.

MRS LINDEN The great thing? What do you mean?

NORA I know you look down upon me, Christina; but you have no right to. You are proud of having worked so hard and so long for your mother.

MRS LINDEN I am sure I don't look down upon anyone; but it's true I am both proud and glad when I remember that I was able to keep my mother's last days free from care.

NORA And you're proud to think of what you have done for your brothers, too.

MRS LINDEN Have I not the right to be?

NORA Yes, surely. But now let me tell you, Christina... I, too, have something to be proud and glad of.

MRS LINDEN I don't doubt it. But what do you mean?

NORA Hush! Not so loud. Only think, if Torvald were to hear! He mustn't... not for worlds! No one must know about it, Christina... no one but you.

MRS LINDEN Why, what can it be?

NORA Come over here. [*Draws her down beside her on the sofa.*]
Yes, Christina... I, too, have something to be proud and glad of.
I saved Torvald's life.

Mrs LINDEN Saved his life? How?

NORA I told you about our going to Italy. Torvald would have died
but for that.

Mrs LINDEN Well... and your father gave you the money.

NORA [*Smiling.*] Yes, so Torvald and everyone believes; but...

Mrs LINDEN But...?

NORA Papa didn't give us one penny. It was I that found
the money.

Mrs LINDEN You? All that money?

NORA Twelve hundred dollars. Four thousand eight hundred
crowns. What do you say to that?

Mrs LINDEN My dear Nora, how did you manage it? Did you win
it in the lottery?

NORA [*Contemptuously.*] In the lottery? Pooh! Any fool could have
done that!

Mrs LINDEN Then where ever did you get it from?

NORA [*Hums and smiles mysteriously.*] Hm; tra-la-la-la!

Mrs LINDEN Of course, you couldn't borrow it.

NORA No? Why not?

MRS LINDEN Why, a wife can't borrow without her husband's consent.

NORA [*Tossing her head.*] Oh! When the wife has some idea of business, and knows how to set about things...

MRS LINDEN But, Nora, I don't understand...

NORA Well, you needn't. I never said I borrowed the money. There are many ways I may have got it. [*Throws herself back on the sofa.*] I may have got it from some admirer. When one is so... attractive as I am...

MRS LINDEN You're too silly, Nora.

NORA Now I'm sure you're dying of curiosity, Christina...

MRS LINDEN Listen to me, Nora dear: haven't you been a little rash?

NORA [*Sitting upright again.*] Is it rash to save one's husband's life?

MRS LINDEN I think it was rash of you, without his knowledge...

NORA But it would have been fatal for him to know! Can't you understand that? He wasn't even to suspect how ill he was. The doctors came to me privately and told me his life was in danger... that nothing could save him but a winter in the South. Do you think I didn't try diplomacy first? I told him how I longed to have a trip abroad, like other young wives; I wept and prayed; I said he ought to think of my condition, and not to thwart me; and then I hinted that he could borrow the money. But then, Christina, he got almost angry. He said I was frivolous, and that it was his duty as a husband not to yield to my whims and fancies... so he called them. Very well, thought I, but saved you must be; and then I found the way to do it.

Mrs LINDEN And did your husband never learn from your father that the money was not from him?

NORA No; never. Papa died at that very time. I meant to have told him all about it, and begged him to say nothing. But he was so ill... unhappily, it wasn't necessary.

Mrs LINDEN And you have never confessed to your husband?

NORA Good heavens! What can you be thinking of of? Tell him when he has such a loathing of debt. And besides... how painful and humiliating it would be for Torvald, with his manly self-respect, to know that he owed anything to me! It would utterly upset the relation between us; our beautiful, happy home would never again be what it is.

Mrs LINDEN Will you never tell him?

NORA [*Thoughtfully, half-smiling.*] Yes, some time perhaps... many, many years hence, when I'm... not so pretty. You mustn't laugh at me! Of course, I mean when Torvald is not so much in love with me as he is now; when it doesn't amuse him any longer to see me dancing about, and dressing up and acting. Then it might be well to have something in reserve. [*Breaking off.*] Nonsense! nonsense! That time will never come. Now, what do you say to my grand secret, Christina? Am I fit for nothing now? You may believe it has cost me a lot of anxiety. It has been no joke to meet my engagements punctually. You must know, Christina, that in business there are things called instalments, and quarterly interest, that are terribly hard to provide for. So I've had to pinch a little here and there, wherever I could. I couldn't save much out of the housekeeping, for, of course, Torvald had to live well. And I couldn't let the children go about badly dressed; all I got for them, I spent on them, the darlings!

MRS LINDEN Poor Nora! So it had to come out of your own pocket money.

NORA Yes, of course. After all, the whole thing was my doing. When Torvald gave me money for clothes, and so on, I never spent more than half of it; I always bought the simplest and cheapest things. It's a mercy that everything suits me so well... Torvald never had any suspicions. But it was often very hard, Christina dear. For it's nice to be beautifully dressed... now, isn't it?

MRS LINDEN Indeed it is.

NORA Well, and besides that, I made money in other ways. Last winter I was so lucky... I got a heap of copying to do. I shut myself up every evening and wrote far into the night. Oh, sometimes I was so tired, so tired. And yet it was splendid to work in that way and earn money. I almost felt as if I was a man.

MRS LINDEN Then how much have you been able to pay off?

NORA Well, I can't precisely say. It's difficult to keep that sort of business clear. I only know that I've paid everything I could scrape together. Sometimes I really didn't know where to turn. [*Smiles.*] Then I used to sit here and pretend that a rich old gentleman was in love with me...

MRS LINDEN What! What gentleman?

NORA Oh, nobody!... that he was dead now, and that when his will was opened, there stood in large letters: "Pay over at once everything of which I die possessed to that charming person, Mrs Nora Helmer."

MRS LINDEN But, my dear Nora... what gentleman do you mean?

NORA Oh dear, can't you understand? There wasn't any old gentleman: it was only what I used to dream and dream when I was at my wits' end for money. But it doesn't matter now... the tiresome old creature may stay where he is for me. I care nothing for him or his will; for now my troubles are over. [*Springing up.*] Oh, Christina, how glorious it is to think of! Free from all anxiety! Free, quite free. To be able to play and romp about with the children; to have things tasteful and pretty in the house, exactly as Torvald likes it! And then the spring will soon be here, with the great blue sky. Perhaps then we shall have a little holiday. Perhaps I shall see the sea again. Oh, what a wonderful thing it is to live and to be happy!

[*The hall doorbell rings.*]

MRS LINDEN [*Rising.*] There's a ring. Perhaps I had better go.

NORA No; do stay. No one will come here. It's sure to be someone for Torvald.

ELLEN [*In the doorway.*] If you please, ma'am, there's a gentleman to speak to Mr Helmer.

NORA Who is the gentleman?

KROGSTAD [*In the doorway.*] It is I, Mrs Helmer.

[*Mrs LINDEN starts and turns away to the window.*]

NORA [*Goes a step towards him, anxiously, speaking low.*] You? What is it? What do you want with my husband?

KROGSTAD Bank business... in a way. I hold a small post in the Joint Stock Bank, and your husband is to be our new chief, I hear.

NORA Then it is…?

KROGSTAD Only tiresome business, Mrs Helmer; nothing more.

NORA Then will you please go to his study.

[*KROGSTAD goes. She bows indifferently while she closes the door into the hall. Then she goes to the stove and looks to the fire.*]

MRS LINDEN Nora… who was that man?

NORA A Mr Krogstad… a lawyer.

MRS LINDEN Then it was really he?

NORA Do you know him?

MRS LINDEN I used to know him… many years ago. He was in a lawyer's office in our town.

NORA Yes, so he was.

MRS LINDEN How he has changed!

NORA I believe his marriage was unhappy.

MRS LINDEN And he is a widower now?

NORA With a lot of children. There! Now it will burn up. [*She closes the stove, and pushes the rocking chair a little aside.*]

MRS LINDEN His business is not of the most creditable, they say?

NORA Isn't it? I daresay not. I don't know. But don't let us think of business… it's so tiresome.

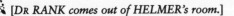

[Dr RANK *comes out of* HELMER's *room.*]

RANK [*Still in the doorway.*] No, no; I'm in your way. I shall go and have a chat with your wife. [*Shuts the door and sees* MRS LINDEN] Oh, I beg your pardon. I'm in the way here too.

NORA No, not in the least. [*Introduces them.*] Doctor Rank – Mrs Linden.

RANK Oh, indeed; I've often heard Mrs Linden's name; I think I passed you on the stairs as I came up.

MRS LINDEN Yes, I go so very slowly. Stairs try me so much.

RANK Ah... you are not very strong?

MRS LINDEN Only overworked.

RANK Nothing more? Then no doubt you've come to town to find rest in a round of dissipation?

MRS LINDEN I have come to look for employment.

RANK Is that an approved remedy for overwork?

MRS LINDEN One must live, Doctor Rank.

RANK Yes, that seems to be the general opinion.

NORA Come, Doctor Rank... you yourself want to live.

RANK To be sure I do. However wretched I may be, I want to drag on as long as possible. All my patients, too, have the same mania. And it's the same with people whose complaint is moral. At this very moment Helmer is talking to just such a wreck as I mean.

Mrs LINDEN [*Softly.*] Ah!

NORA Whom do you mean?

RANK Oh, a fellow named Krogstad, a man you know nothing about… corrupt to the very core of his character. But even he began by announcing, as a matter of vast importance, that he must live.

NORA Indeed? And what did he want with Torvald?

RANK I haven't an idea; I only gathered that it was some bank business.

NORA I didn't know that Krog… that this Mr Krogstad had anything to do with the Bank?

RANK Yes. He has some sort of place there. [*To Mrs LINDEN.*] I don't know whether in your part of the country, you have people who go grubbing and sniffing around in search of moral rottenness… whose policy it is to fill good places with men of tainted character who they can keep under their eye and in their power. Honest men they leave out in the cold.

Mrs LINDEN Well, I suppose the… delicate characters require most care.

RANK [*Shrugs his shoulders.*] There we have it! It's that notion that makes society a hospital.

[*NORA, deep in her own thoughts, breaks into half-stifled laughter and claps her hands.*]

RANK Why do you laugh at that? Have you any idea what "society" is?

NORA What do I care for your tiresome society? I was laughing at something else... something excessively amusing. Tell me, Doctor Rank, are all the employees at the Bank dependent on Torvald now?

RANK Is that what strikes you as awfully amusing?

NORA [*Smiles and hums.*] Never mind, never mind! [*Walks about the room.*] Yes, it is funny to think that we... that Torvald has such power over so many people. [*Takes the bag from her pocket.*] Doctor Rank, will you have a macaroon?

RANK Oh, dear, dear... macaroons! I thought they were contraband here.

NORA Yes; but Christina brought me these.

MRS LINDEN What! I...?

NORA Oh, well! Don't be frightened. You couldn't possibly know that Torvald had forbidden them. The fact is, he's afraid of me spoiling my teeth. But, oh bother, just for once!... That's for you, Doctor Rank! [*Puts a macaroon into his mouth.*] And you too, Christina. And I'll have one while we're about it... only a tiny one, or at most two. [*Walks about again.*] Oh dear, I am happy! There's only one thing in the world I really want.

RANK Well; what's that?

NORA There's something I should so like to say... in Torvald's hearing.

RANK Then why don't you say it?

NORA Because I daren't, it's so ugly.

Mrs LINDEN Ugly!

RANK In that case you'd better not. But to us you might… What is it you would so like to say in Helmer's hearing?

NORA I should so love to say, "Damn it all!*"

RANK Are you out of your mind?

Mrs LINDEN Good gracious, Nora…!

RANK Say it… there he is!

NORA [*Hides the macaroons.*] Hush-sh-sh!

[*HELMER comes out of his room, hat in hand, with his overcoat on his arm.*]

NORA [*Going towards him.*] Well, Torvald dear, have you got rid of him?

HELMER Yes; he has just gone.

NORA Let me introduce you… this is Christina, who has come to town…

HELMER Christina? Pardon me, I don't know…

NORA Mrs Linden, Torvald dear… Christina Linden.

HELMER [*To Mrs LINDEN.*] Indeed! A schoolfriend of my wife's, no doubt?

* **Dod og pine,** *literally "death and torture"; but by usage a comparatively mild oath.*

Mrs LINDEN Yes; we knew each other as girls.

NORA And only think! She has taken this long journey on purpose to speak to you.

HELMER To speak to me!

Mrs LINDEN Well, not quite...

NORA You see, Christina is tremendously clever at office work, and she's so anxious to work under a first-rate man of business in order to learn still more...

HELMER [*To Mrs LINDEN.*] Very sensible indeed.

NORA And when she heard you were appointed manager... it was telegraphed, you know... she started off at once, and... Torvald, dear, for my sake, you must do something for Christina. Now can't you?

HELMER It's not impossible. I presume Mrs Linden is a widow?

Mrs LINDEN Yes.

HELMER And you have already had some experience of business?

Mrs LINDEN A good deal.

HELMER Well, then, it's very likely I may be able to find a place for you.

NORA [*Clapping her hands.*] There now! There now!

HELMER You have come at a fortunate moment, Mrs Linden.

MRS LINDEN Oh, how can I thank you…?

HELMER [*Smiling.*] There is no occasion. [*Puts on his overcoat.*] But for the present you must excuse me…

RANK Wait; I am going with you. [*Fetches his fur coat from the hall and warms it at the fire.*]

NORA Don't be long, Torvald dear.

HELMER Only an hour; not more.

NORA Are you going too, Christina?

MRS LINDEN [*Putting on her walking things.*] Yes, I must set about looking for lodgings.

HELMER Then perhaps we can go together?

NORA [*Helping her.*] What a pity we haven't a spare room for you; but it's impossible…

MRS LINDEN I shouldn't think of troubling you. Goodbye, dear Nora, and thank you for all your kindness.

NORA Goodbye for the present. Of course, you'll come back this evening. And you, too, Doctor Rank. What! If you're well enough? Of course you'll be well enough. Only wrap up warmly. [*They go out, talking, into the hall. Outside on the stairs are heard children's voices.*] There they are! There they are! [*She runs to the outer door and opens it. The nurse, ANNA, enters the hall with the children.*] Come in! Come in! [*Stoops down and kisses the children.*] Oh, my sweet darlings! Do you see them, Christina? Aren't they lovely?

RANK Don't let us stand here chattering in the draught.

HELMER Come, Mrs Linden; only mothers can stand such a temperature.

[DR RANK, HELMER and MRS LINDEN go down the stairs; ANNA enters the room with the children; NORA also, shutting the door.]

NORA How fresh and bright you look! And what red cheeks you've got! Like apples and roses. [*The children chatter to her during what follows.*] Have you had great fun? That's splendid! Oh, really! You've been giving Emmy and Bob a ride on your sledge!... both at once, only think! Why, you're quite a man, Ivar. Oh, give her to me a little, Anna. My sweet little dolly! [*Takes the smallest from the nurse and dances with her.*] Yes, yes; mother will dance with Bob too. What! Did you have a game of snowballs? Oh, I wish I'd been there. No, leave them, Anna; I'll take their things off. Oh, yes, let me do it; it's such fun. Go to the nursery; you look frozen. You'll find some hot coffee on the stove.

[*The NURSE goes into the room on the left. NORA takes off the children's things and throws them down anywhere, while the children talk all together.*] Really! A big dog ran after you? But he didn't bite you? No; dogs don't bite dear little dolly children. Don't peep into those parcels, Ivar. What is it? Wouldn't you like to know? Take care... it'll bite! What? Shall we have a game? What shall we play at? Hide-and-seek? Yes, let's play hide-and-seek. Bob shall hide first. Am I to? Yes, let me hide first.

[*She and the children play, with laughter and shouting, in the room and the adjacent one to the right. At last NORA hides under the table; the children come rushing in, look for her, but cannot find her, hear her half-choked laughter, rush to the table, lift up the cover and see her. Loud shouts. She creeps out, as though to frighten them. Fresh shouts. Meanwhile, there has been a knock at the door leading into the hall. No one has heard it. Now the door is half opened and KROGSTAD appears. He waits a little; the game is renewed.*]

KROGSTAD I beg your pardon, Mrs Helmer…

NORA [*With a suppressed cry, turns round and half jumps up.*] Ah! What do you want?

KROGSTAD Excuse me; the outer door was ajar… somebody must have forgotten to shut it…

NORA [*Standing up.*] My husband is not at home, Mr Krogstad.

KROGSTAD I know it.

NORA Then what do you want here?

KROGSTAD To say a few words to you.

NORA To me? [*To the children, softly.*] Go in to Anna. What? No, the strange man won't hurt mamma. When he's gone we'll go on playing. [*She leads the children into the left-hand room and shuts the door behind them. Uneasy, in suspense.*] It is to me you wish to speak?

KROGSTAD Yes, to you.

NORA Today? But it's not the first yet…

KROGSTAD No, today is Christmas Eve. It will depend upon yourself whether you have a merry Christmas.

NORA What do you want? I'm not ready today…

KROGSTAD Never mind that just now. I have come about another matter. You have a minute to spare?

NORA Oh, yes, I suppose so; although...

KROGSTAD Good. I was sitting in the restaurant opposite, and I saw your husband go down the street...

NORA Well?

KROGSTAD ...with a lady.

NORA What then?

KROGSTAD May I ask if the lady was a Mrs Linden?

NORA Yes.

KROGSTAD Who has just come to town?

NORA Yes. Today.

KROGSTAD I believe she is an intimate friend of yours.

NORA Certainly. But I don't understand...

KROGSTAD I used to know her too.

NORA I know you did.

KROGSTAD Ah! You know all about it. I thought as much. Now, frankly, is Mrs Linden to have a place in the Bank?

NORA How dare you catechise me in this way, Mr Krogstad... you, a subordinate of my husband's? But since you ask, you shall know. Yes, Mrs Linden is to be employed. And it is I who recommended her, Mr Krogstad. Now you know.

KROGSTAD Then my guess was right.

NORA [*Walking up and down.*] You see one has a wee bit of influence, after all. It doesn't follow because one's only a woman… When people are in a subordinate position, Mr Krogstad, they ought really to be careful how they offend anybody who… hm…

KROGSTAD …who has influence?

NORA Exactly.

KROGSTAD [*Taking another tone.*] Mrs Helmer, will you have the kindness to employ your influence on my behalf?

NORA What? How do you mean?

KROGSTAD Will you be so good as to see that I retain my subordinate position in the Bank?

NORA What do you mean? Who wants to take it from you?

KROGSTAD Oh, you needn't pretend ignorance. I can very well understand that it cannot be pleasant for your friend to meet me; and I can also understand now for whose sake I am to be hounded out.

NORA But I assure you…

KROGSTAD Come come now, once for all: there is time yet, and I advise you to use your influence to prevent it.

NORA But, Mr Krogstad, I have no influence… absolutely none.

KROGSTAD None? I thought you said a moment ago...

NORA Of course, not in that sense. I! How can you imagine that I should have any such influence over my husband?

KROGSTAD Oh, I know your husband from our college days. I don't think he is any more inflexible than other husbands.

NORA If you talk disrespectfully of my husband, I must request you to leave the house.

KROGSTAD You are bold, madam.

NORA I am afraid of you no longer. When New Year's Day is over, I shall soon be out of the whole business.

KROGSTAD [*Controlling himself.*] Listen to me, Mrs Helmer. If need be, I shall fight as though for my life to keep my little place in the Bank.

NORA Yes, so it seems.

KROGSTAD It's not only for the salary: that is what I care least about. It's something else... Well, I had better make a clean breast of it. Of course, you know, like every one else, that some years ago I... got into trouble.

NORA I think I've heard something of the sort.

KROGSTAD The matter never came into court; but from that moment all paths were barred to me. Then I took up the business you know about. I had to turn my hand to something; and I don't think I've been one of the worst. But now I must get clear of it all. My sons are growing up; for their sake I must try to recover my character as well as I can. This place in the Bank was the first step;

and now your husband wants to kick me off the ladder, back into the mire.

NORA But I assure you, Mr Krogstad, I haven't the least power to help you.

KROGSTAD That is because you have not the will, but I can compel you.

NORA You won't tell my husband that I owe you money?

KROGSTAD Hm; suppose I were to?

NORA It would be shameful of you. [*With tears in her voice.*] The secret that is my joy and my pride… that he should learn it in such an ugly, coarse way… and from you. It would involve me in all sorts of unpleasantness…

KROGSTAD Only unpleasantness?

NORA [*Hotly.*] But just do it. It's you that will come off worst, for then my husband will see what a bad man you are, and then you certainly won't keep your place.

KROGSTAD I asked whether it was only domestic unpleasantness you feared?

NORA If my husband gets to know about it, he will, of course, pay you off at once, and then we shall have nothing more to do with you.

KROGSTAD [*Coming a pace nearer.*] Listen, Mrs Helmer: either your memory is defective, or you don't know much about business. I must make the position clear to you.

NORA How so?

KROGSTAD When your husband was ill, you came to me to borrow twelve hundred dollars.

NORA I knew of nobody else.

KROGSTAD I promised to find you the money...

NORA And you did find it.

KROGSTAD I promised to find you the money, on certain conditions. You were so much taken up at the time about your husband's illness, and so eager to have the wherewithal for your journey, that you probably did not give much thought to the details. Allow me to remind you of them. I promised to find you the amount in exchange for a note of hand, which I drew up.

NORA Yes, and I signed it.

KROGSTAD Quite right. But then I added a few lines, making your father security for the debt. Your father was to sign this.

NORA Was to...? He did sign it!

KROGSTAD I had left the date blank. That is to say, your father was himself to date his signature. Do you recollect that?

NORA Yes, I believe...

KROGSTAD Then I gave you the paper to send to your father, by post. Is not that so?

NORA Yes.

KROGSTAD And, of course, you did so at once; for within five or six days you brought me back the document with your father's signature; and I handed you the money.

NORA Well? Have I not made my payments punctually?

KROGSTAD Fairly... yes. But to return to the point: You were in great trouble at the time, Mrs Helmer.

NORA I was indeed!

KROGSTAD Your father was very ill, I believe?

NORA He was on his death bed.

KROGSTAD And died soon after?

NORA Yes.

KROGSTAD Tell me, Mrs Helmer: do you happen to recollect the day of his death? The day of the month, I mean?

NORA Father died on the 29th of September.

KROGSTAD Quite correct. I have made inquiries. And here comes in the remarkable point... [*produces a paper*] which I cannot explain.

NORA What remarkable point? I don't know...

KROGSTAD The remarkable point, madam, that your father signed this paper three days after his death!

NORA What! I don't understand...

KROGSTAD Your father died on the 29th of September. But look here: he has dated his signature October 2nd! Is not that remarkable? Mrs Helmer? [*NORA is silent.*] Can you explain it? [*NORA stays silent.*] It is noteworthy, too, that the words "October 2nd" and the year are not in your father's handwriting, but in one which I believe I know. Well, this may be explained; your father may have forgotten to date his signature, and somebody may have added the date at random, before the fact of your father's death was known. There is nothing wrong in that. Everything depends on the signature. Of course it is genuine, Mrs Helmer? It was really your father, who with his own hand, wrote his name here?

NORA [*After a short silence, throws her head back and looks defiantly at him.*] No, it was not. I wrote father's name.

KROGSTAD Ah!… Are you aware, madam, that that is a dangerous admission?

NORA How so? You will soon get your money.

KROGSTAD May I ask you one more question? Why did you not send the paper to your father?

NORA It was impossible. Father was ill. If I had asked him for his signature, I should have had to tell him why I wanted the money, but he was so ill I really could not tell him that my husband's life was in danger. It was impossible.

KROGSTAD Then it would have been better to have given up your tour.

NORA No, I couldn't do that; my husband's life depended on that journey. I couldn't give it up.

KROGSTAD And did it never occur to you that you were playing me false?

NORA That was nothing to me. I didn't care in the least about you. I couldn't endure you for all the cruel difficulties you made, although you knew how ill my husband was.

KROGSTAD Mrs Helmer, you evidently do not realize what you have been guilty of. But I can assure you it was nothing more and nothing worse that made me an outcast from society.

NORA You! You want me to believe that you did a brave thing to save your wife's life?

KROGSTAD The law takes no account of motives.

NORA Then it must be a very bad law.

KROGSTAD Bad or not, if I produce this document in court, you will be condemned according to law.

NORA I don't believe that. Do you mean to tell me that a daughter has no right to spare her dying father trouble and anxiety?… that a wife has no right to save her husband's life? I don't know much about the law, but I'm sure you'll find, somewhere or another, that that is allowed. And you don't know that… you, a lawyer! You must be a bad one, Mr Krogstad.

KROGSTAD Possibly. But business… such business as ours… I do understand. You believe that? Very well; now do as you please. But this I may tell you, that if I am flung into the gutter a second time, you shall keep me company.

[*Bows and goes out through hall.*]

NORA [*Stands a while thinking, then tosses her head.*] Oh
nonsense! He wants to frighten me. I'm not so foolish as that.
[*Begins folding the children's clothes. Pauses.*] But...? No, it's
impossible! Why, I did it for love!

CHILDREN [*At the door, left.*] Mamma, the strange man has
gone now.

NORA Yes, yes, I know. But don't tell anyone about the strange
man. Do you hear? Not even papa!

CHILDREN No, mamma; and now will you play with us again?

NORA No, no, not now.

CHILDREN Oh, do, mamma; you know you promised.

NORA Yes, but I can't just now. Run to the nursery; I have so
much to do. Run along, run along, and be good, my darlings! [*She
pushes them gently into the inner room, and closes the door behind
them. Sits on the sofa, embroiders a few stitches, but soon pauses.*]
No! [*Throws down the work, rises, goes to the hall door and calls
out.*] Ellen, bring in the Christmas tree! [*Goes to table, left, and
opens the drawer, again pauses.*] No, it's quite impossible!

ELLEN [*With Christmas tree.*] Where shall I stand it, ma'am?

NORA There, in the middle of the room.

ELLEN Shall I bring in anything else?

NORA No, thank you, I have all I want.

[*ELLEN, having put down the tree, goes out.*]

NORA [*Busy dressing the tree.*] There must be a candle here... and flowers there... That horrible man! Nonsense, nonsense! There's nothing to be afraid of. The Christmas tree shall be beautiful. I'll do everything to please you, Torvald; I'll sing and dance... sing and dance...

[*Enter HELMER by the hall door, with a bundle of documents.*]

NORA Oh! You're back already?

HELMER Yes. Has anybody been here?

NORA No.

HELMER That's odd. I saw Krogstad come out of the house.

NORA Did you? Oh, yes, by the bye, he was here for a minute.

HELMER Nora, I can see by your manner that he has been begging you to put in a good word for him.

NORA Yes.

HELMER And you were to do it as if of your own accord? You were to say nothing to me of his having been here. Didn't he suggest that too?

NORA Yes, Torvald, but...

HELMER Nora, Nora! And you could condescend to that! To speak to such a man, to make him a promise! And then to tell me an untruth about it!

NORA An untruth!

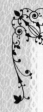

HELMER Didn't you say that nobody had been here? [*Pointing his finger.*] My little bird must never do that again! A song bird must sing clear and true; no false notes. [*Puts his arm round her.*] That's so, isn't it? Yes, I was sure of it. [*Lets her go.*] And now we'll say no more about it. [*Sits down before the fire.*] Oh, how cosy and quiet it is here! [*Glances into his documents.*]

NORA [*Busy with the tree, after a short silence.*] Torvald!

HELMER Yes.

NORA I'm looking forward so much to the Stenborgs' fancy ball the day after tomorrow.

HELMER And I'm on tenterhooks to see what surprise you have in store for me.

NORA Oh, it's too tiresome!

HELMER What is?

NORA I can't think of anything good. Everything seems so foolish and meaningless.

HELMER Has little Nora made that discovery?

NORA [*Behind his chair, with her arms on the back.*] Are you very busy, Torvald?

HELMER Well...

NORA What papers are those?

HELMER Bank business.

NORA Already!

HELMER I have got the retiring manager to let me make some necessary changes in the staff and the organization. I can do this during Christmas week. I want to have everything straight by the New Year.

NORA Then that's why that poor Krogstad…

HELMER Hm.

NORA [*Still leaning over the chair-back and slowly stroking his hair.*] If you hadn't been so very busy, I should have asked you a great, great favour, Torvald.

HELMER What can it be? Out with it.

NORA Nobody has such perfect taste as you, and I should so love to look well at the fancy ball. Torvald, dear, couldn't you take me in hand, and settle what I'm to be, and arrange my costume for me?

HELMER Aha! So my wilful little woman is at a loss, and making signals of distress.

NORA Yes, please, Torvald. I can't get on without your help.

HELMER Well, well, I'll think it over, and we'll soon hit upon something.

NORA Oh, how good that is of you! [*Goes to the tree again; pause.*] How well the red flowers show… Tell me, was it anything so very dreadful this Krogstad got into trouble about?

HELMER Forgery, that's all. Don't you know what that means?

NORA Mayn't he have been driven to it by need?

HELMER Yes; or, like so many others, he may have done it in pure heedlessness. I am not so hard-hearted as to condemn a man absolutely for a single fault.

NORA No, surely not, Torvald!

HELMER Many a man can retrieve his character, if he owns his crime and takes the punishment.

NORA Punishment...?

HELMER But Krogstad didn't do that. He evaded the law by means of tricks and subterfuges; and that is what has morally ruined him.

NORA Do you think that...?

HELMER Just think how a man with a thing of that sort on his conscience must be always lying and canting and shamming. Think of the mask he must wear even towards those who stand nearest him... towards his own wife and children. The effect on the children... that's the most terrible part of it, Nora.

NORA Why?

HELMER Because in such an atmosphere of lies home life is poisoned and contaminated in every fibre. Every breath the children draw contains some germ of evil.

NORA [*Closer behind him.*] Are you sure of that?

HELMER As a lawyer, my dear, I have seen it often enough. Nearly all cases of early corruption may be traced to lying mothers.

NORA Why... mothers?

HELMER It generally comes from the mother's side; but, of course, the father's influence may act in the same way. Every lawyer knows it too well. And here has this Krogstad been poisoning his own children for years past by a life of lies and hypocrisy... that is why I call him morally ruined. [*Holds out both hands to her.*] So my sweet little Nora must promise not to plead his cause. Shake hands upon it. Come, come, what's this? Give me your hand. That's right. Then it's a bargain. I assure you it would have been impossible for me to work with him. It gives me a positive sense of physical discomfort to come in contact with such people.

[*NORA draws her hand away, and moves to the other side of the Christmas tree.*]

NORA How warm it is here. And I have so much to do.

HELMER [*Rises and gathers up his papers.*] Yes, and I must try to get some of these papers looked through before dinner. And I shall think over your costume too. Perhaps I may even find something to hang in gilt paper on the Christmas tree... [*Lays his hand on her head.*] My precious little song bird!

[*He goes into his room and shuts the door.*]

NORA [*Softly, after a pause.*] It can't be. It's impossible. It must be impossible!

ANNA [*At the door, left.*] The little ones are begging so prettily to come to mamma.

NORA No, no, no; don't let them come to me! Keep them with you, Anna.

ANNA Very well, ma'am.

[*Shuts the door.*]

NORA [*Pale with terror.*] Corrupt my children!… Poison my home!
[*Short pause. She throws back her head.*] It's not true! It can never,
never be true!

ACT SECOND

The same room. In the corner, beside the piano, stands the Christmas tree, stripped, and with the candles burnt out. NORA's outdoor things lie on the sofa.

NORA, alone, is walking about restlessly. At last she stops by the sofa, takes up her cloak, then lays it down again.

NORA There's somebody coming! [*Goes to the hall door and listens.*] Nobody; of course, nobody will come today, Christmas day; nor tomorrow either. But perhaps... [*Opens the door and looks out.*] No, nothing in the letter box; quite empty. [*Comes forward.*] Stuff and nonsense! Of course, he won't really do anything. Such a thing couldn't happen. It's impossible! Why, I have three little children.

[*ANNA enters from the left, with a large cardboard box.*]

ANNA I've found the box with the fancy dress at last.

NORA Thanks; put it down on the table.

ANNA [*Does so.*] But I'm afraid it's very much out of order.

NORA Oh, I wish I could tear it into a hundred thousand pieces!

ANNA Oh, no. It can easily be put to rights... just a little patience.

NORA I shall go and get Mrs Linden to help me.

ANNA Going out again? In such weather as this! You'll catch cold, ma'am, and be ill.

NORA Worse things might happen... What are the children doing?

ANNA They're playing with their Christmas presents, poor little dears, but...

NORA Do they often ask for me?

ANNA You see they've been so used to having their mamma with them.

NORA Yes; but, Anna, I can't have them so much with me in future.

ANNA Well, little children get used to anything.

NORA Do you think they do? Do you believe they would forget their mother if she went quite away?

ANNA Gracious me! Quite away?

NORA Tell me, Anna... I've so often wondered about it... how could you bring yourself to give your child up to strangers?

ANNA I had to when I came to nurse my little Miss Nora.

NORA But how could you make up your mind to it?

ANNA When I had the chance of such a good place? A poor girl who's been in trouble must take what comes. That wicked man did nothing for me.

NORA But your daughter must have forgotten you.

ANNA Oh, no, ma'am, that she hasn't. She wrote to me both when she was confirmed and when she was married.

NORA [*Embracing her.*] Dear old Anna... you were a good mother to me when I was little.

ANNA My poor little Nora had no mother but me.

NORA And if my little ones had nobody else, I'm sure you would... Nonsense, nonsense! [*Opens the box.*] Go in to the children. Now I must... You'll see how lovely I shall be tomorrow.

ANNA I'm sure there will be no one at the ball so lovely as my Miss Nora.

[*She goes into the room on the left.*]

NORA [*Takes the costume out of the box, but soon throws it down again.*] Oh, if I dared go out. If only nobody would come. If only nothing would happen here in the meantime. Rubbish; nobody is coming. Only not to think. What a delicious muff! Beautiful gloves, beautiful gloves! To forget... to forget! One, two, three, four, five, six... [*With a scream.*] Ah, there they come. [*Goes towards the door, then stands irresolute.*]

[*Mrs LINDEN enters from the hall, where she has taken off her things.*]

NORA Oh, it's you, Christina. There's nobody else there? I'm so glad you have come.

MRS LINDEN I hear you called at my lodgings.

NORA Yes, I was just passing. There's something you must help me with. Let us sit here on the sofa so. Tomorrow evening there's to be a fancy ball at Consul Stenborg's overhead, and Torvald wants me to appear as a Neapolitan fisher-girl, and dance the tarantella; I learned it at Capri.

Mrs LINDEN I see... quite a performance.

NORA Yes, Torvald wishes it. Look, this is the costume; Torvald had it made for me in Italy. But now it's all so torn, I don't know...

Mrs LINDEN Oh, we shall soon set that to rights. It's only the trimming that has come loose here and there. Have you a needle and thread? Ah, here's the very thing.

NORA Oh, how kind of you.

Mrs LINDEN [*Sewing.*] So you're to be in costume tomorrow, Nora? I'll tell you what... I shall come in for a moment to see you in all your glory. But I've quite forgotten to thank you for the pleasant evening yesterday.

NORA [*Rises and walks across the room.*] Oh, yesterday, it didn't seem so pleasant as usual... You should have come to town a little sooner, Christina... Torvald has certainly the art of making home bright and beautiful.

Mrs LINDEN You too, I should think, or you wouldn't be your father's daughter. But tell me... is Doctor Rank always so depressed as he was yesterday evening?

NORA No, yesterday it was particularly noticeable. You see, he suffers from a dreadful illness. He has spinal consumption, poor fellow. They say his father was a horrible man, who kept mistresses and all sorts of things... so the son has been sickly from his childhood, you understand.

MRS LINDEN [*Lets her sewing fall into her lap.*] Why, my darling Nora, how do you come to know such things?

NORA [*Moving about the room.*] Oh, when one has three children, one sometimes has visits from women who are half… half doctors… and they talk of one thing and another.

MRS LINDEN [*Goes on sewing; a short pause.*] Does Doctor Rank come here every day?

NORA Every day of his life. He has been Torvald's most intimate friend from boyhood, and he's a good friend of mine too. Doctor Rank is quite one of the family.

MRS LINDEN But tell me… is he quite sincere? I mean, isn't he rather given to flattering people?

NORA No, quite the contrary. Why should you think so?

MRS LINDEN When you introduced us yesterday he said he had often heard my name; but I noticed afterwards that your husband had no notion who I was. How could Doctor Rank…?

NORA He was quite right, Christina. You see, Torvald loves me so indescribably, he wants to have me all to himself, as he says. When we were first married he was almost jealous if I even mentioned any of my old friends at home; so naturally I gave up doing it. But I often talk of the old times to Doctor Rank, for he likes to hear about them.

MRS LINDEN Listen to me, Nora! You are still a child in many ways. I am older than you, and have had more experience. I'll tell you something? You ought to get clear of all this with Dr Rank.

NORA Get clear of what?

MRS LINDEN The whole affair, I should say. You were talking yesterday of a rich admirer who was to find you money...

NORA Yes, one who never existed, worst luck. What then?

MRS LINDEN Has Doctor Rank money?

NORA Yes, he has.

MRS LINDEN And nobody to provide for?

NORA Nobody. But...?

MRS LINDEN And he comes here every day?

NORA Yes, I told you so.

MRS LINDEN I should have thought he would have had better taste.

NORA I don't understand you a bit.

MRS LINDEN Don't pretend, Nora. Do you suppose I can't guess who lent you the twelve hundred dollars?

NORA Are you out of your senses? How can you think such a thing? A friend who comes here every day! Why, the position would be unbearable!

MRS LINDEN Then it really is not he?

NORA No, I assure you. It never for a moment occurred to me... Besides, at that time he had nothing to lend; he came into his property afterwards.

MRS LINDEN Well, I believe that was lucky for you, Nora dear.

NORA No, really, it would never have struck me to ask Dr Rank…
And yet, I'm certain that if I did…

MRS LINDEN But of course you never would.

NORA Of course not. It's inconceivable that it should ever be
necessary. But I'm quite sure that if I spoke to Doctor Rank…

MRS LINDEN Behind your husband's back?

NORA I must get clear of the other thing; that's behind his back
too. I must get clear of that.

MRS LINDEN Yes, yes, I told you so yesterday, but…

NORA [*Walking up and down.*] A man can manage these things
much better than a woman.

MRS LINDEN One's own husband, yes.

NORA Nonsense. [*Stands still.*] When everything is paid, one gets
back the paper.

MRS LINDEN Of course.

NORA And can tear it into a hundred thousand pieces, and burn it
up, the nasty, filthy thing!

MRS LINDEN [*Looks at her fixedly, lays down her work, and rises
slowly.*] Nora, you are hiding something from me.

NORA Can you see it in my face?

MRS LINDEN Something has happened since yesterday morning.
Nora, what is it?

NORA [*Going towards her.*] Christina…! [*Listens.*] Hush! There's Torvald coming home. Do you mind going into the nursery for the present? Torvald can't bear to see dressmaking going on. Get Anna to help you.

MRS LINDEN [*Gathers some of the things together.*] Very well, but I shan't go away until you have told me all about it.

[*She goes out to the left, as HELMER enters from the hall.*]

NORA [*Runs to meet him.*] Oh, how I've been longing for you to come, Torvald dear!

HELMER   Was that the dressmaker…?

NORA   No, Christina. She's helping me with my costume. You'll see how nice I shall look.

HELMER   Yes, wasn't that a happy thought of mine?

NORA   Splendid! But isn't it good of me, too, to have given in to you about the tarantella?

HELMER [*Takes her under the chin.*] Good of you! To give in to your own husband? Well well, you little madcap, I know you don't mean it. But I won't disturb you. I daresay you want to be "trying on".

NORA   And you are going to work, I suppose?

HELMER   Yes. [*Shows her a bundle of papers.*] Look here. I've just come from the Bank…

[*Goes towards his room.*]

NORA Torvald.

HELMER [*Stopping.*] Yes?

NORA If your little squirrel were to beg you for something so prettily…

HELMER Well?

NORA Would you do it?

HELMER I must know first what it is.

NORA The squirrel would skip about and play all sorts of tricks if you would only be nice and kind.

HELMER Come, then, out with it.

NORA Your lark would twitter from morning till night…

HELMER Oh, that she does in any case.

NORA I'll be an elf and dance in the moonlight for you, Torvald.

HELMER Nora… you can't mean what you were hinting at this morning?

NORA [*Coming nearer.*] Yes, Torvald, I beg and implore you!

HELMER Have you really the courage to begin that again?

NORA Yes, yes; for my sake, you must let Krogstad keep his place in the Bank.

HELMER My dear Nora, it's his place I intend for Mrs Linden.

NORA Yes, that's so good of you. But instead of Krogstad, you could dismiss some other clerk.

HELMER Why, this is incredible obstinacy! Because you have thoughtlessly promised to put in a word for him, I am to...!

NORA It's not that, Torvald. It's for your own sake. This man writes for the most scurrilous newspapers; you said so yourself. He can do you no end of harm. I'm so terribly afraid of him...

HELMER Ah, I understand; it's old recollections that are frightening you.

NORA What do you mean?

HELMER Of course, you're thinking of your father.

NORA Yes... yes, of course. Only think of the shameful slanders wicked people used to write about father. I believe they would have got him dismissed if you hadn't been sent to look into the thing, and been kind to him, and helped him.

HELMER My little Nora, between your father and me there is all the difference in the world. Your father was not altogether unimpeachable. I am, and I hope to remain so.

NORA Oh, no one knows what wicked men may hit upon. We could live so quietly and happily now, in our cosy, peaceful home, you and I and the children, Torvald! That's why I beg and implore you...

HELMER And it is just by pleading his cause that you make it impossible for me to keep him. It's already known at the Bank that I intend to dismiss Krogstad. If it were now reported that the new manager let himself be turned round his wife's little finger...

NORA What then?

HELMER Oh, nothing, so long as a wilful woman can have her way...! I am to make myself a laughing-stock to the whole staff, and set people saying that I am open to all sorts of outside influence? Take my word for it, I should soon feel the consequences. And besides there is one thing that makes Krogstad impossible for me to work with...

NORA What thing?

HELMER I could perhaps have overlooked his moral failings at a pinch...

NORA Yes, couldn't you, Torvald?

HELMER And I hear he is good at his work. But the fact is, he was a college chum of mine... there was one of those rash friendships between us that one so often repents of later. I may as well confess it at once... he calls me by my Christian name*, and he is tactless enough to do it even when others are present. He delights in putting on airs of familiarity... Torvald here, Torvald there! I assure you it's most painful to me. He would make my position at the Bank perfectly unendurable.

NORA Torvald, surely you're not serious?

HELMER No? Why not?

NORA That's such a petty reason.

HELMER What! Petty! Do you consider me petty!

* *In the original, "We say 'thou' to each other."*

NORA No, on the contrary, Torvald dear, and that's just why...

HELMER Never mind; you call my motives petty; then I must be petty too. Petty! Very well!... Now we'll put an end to this, once and for all. [*Goes to the door into the hall and calls.*] Ellen!

NORA What do you want?

HELMER [*Searching among his papers.*] To settle the thing. [*ELLEN enters.*] Here, take this letter; give it to a messenger. See that he takes it at once. The address is on it. Here's the money.

ELLEN Very well, sir.

[*Goes with the letter.*]

HELMER [*Putting his papers together.*] There, Madam Obstinacy.

NORA [*Breathless.*] Torvald... what was in the letter?

HELMER Krogstad's dismissal.

NORA Call it back again, Torvald! There's still time. Oh, Torvald, call it back again! For my sake, for your own, for the children's sake! Do you hear, Torvald? Do it! You don't know what that letter may bring upon us all.

HELMER Too late.

NORA Yes, too late.

HELMER My dear Nora, I forgive your anxiety, though it's anything but flattering to me. Why should you suppose that I would be afraid of a wretched scribbler's spite? But I forgive you all the same, for it's a proof of your great love for me. [*Takes her in his* *arms.*] That's as it should be, my own dear Nora. Let what will happen... when it comes to the pinch, I shall have strength and courage enough. You shall see: my shoulders are broad enough to bear the whole burden.

NORA [*Terror-struck.*] What do you mean by that?

HELMER The whole burden, I say...

NORA [*With decision.*] That you shall never, never do!

HELMER Very well; then we'll share it, Nora, as man and wife. That is how it should be. [*Petting her.*] Are you satisfied now? Come, come, come, don't look like a scared dove. It's all nothing... fancy. Now you ought to play the tarantella through and practise with the tambourine. I shall sit in my inner room and shut both doors, so that I shall hear nothing. You can make as much noise as you please. [*Turns round in doorway.*] And when Rank comes, just tell him where I'm to be found.

[*He nods to her, and goes with his papers into his room, closing the door.*]

NORA [*Bewildered with terror, stands as though rooted to the ground, and whispers.*] He would do it. Yes, he would do it. He would do it, in spite of all the world... No, never that, never, never! Anything rather than that! Oh, for some way of escape! What shall I do...! [*Hall bell rings.*] Doctor Rank...! Anything, anything, rather than...!

[*NORA draws her hands over her face, pulls herself together, goes to the door and opens it. RANK stands outside hanging up his fur coat. During what follows it begins to grow dark.*]

NORA Good afternoon, Doctor Rank, I knew you by your ring. But you mustn't go to Torvald now. I believe he's busy.

RANK And you?

NORA Oh, you know very well, I have always time for you.

RANK Thank you. I shall avail myself of your kindness as long as I can.

NORA What do you mean? As long as you can?

RANK Yes. Does that frighten you?

NORA I think it's an odd expression. Do you expect anything to happen?

RANK Something I have long been prepared for; but I didn't think it would come so soon.

NORA [*Catching at his arm.*] What have you discovered? Doctor Rank, you must tell me!

RANK [*Sitting down by the stove.*] I am running downhill. There's no help for it.

NORA [*Draws a long breath of relief.*] It's you...?

RANK Who else should it be? Why lie to oneself? I am the most wretched of all my patients, Mrs Helmer. In these last days I have been auditing my life-account – bankrupt! Before a month is over, I shall lie rotting in the churchyard.

NORA Oh! What an ugly way to talk.

RANK The thing itself is so confoundedly ugly, you see. But the worst of it is, so many other ugly things have to be gone through first. There is only one last investigation to be made, and when that is over I shall know pretty certainly when the break-up will begin. There's one thing I want to say to you: Helmer's delicate nature shrinks so from all that is horrible: I will not have him in my sick-room...

NORA But, Doctor Rank...

RANK I won't have him, I say... not on any account! I shall lock my door against him. As soon as I am quite certain of the worst, I shall send you my visiting-card with a black cross on it; and then you will know that the final horror has begun.

NORA Why, you're perfectly unreasonable today; and I did so want you to be in a really good humour.

RANK With death staring me in the face? And to suffer thus for another's sin! Where's the justice of it? And in one way or another you can trace in every family some such inexorable retribution...

NORA [*Stopping her ears.*] Nonsense, nonsense! Now cheer up!

RANK Well, after all, the whole thing's only worth laughing at. My poor innocent spine must do penance for my father's wild oats.

NORA [*At table, left.*] I suppose he was too fond of asparagus and Strasbourg pâté, wasn't he?

RANK Yes; and truffles.

NORA Yes, truffles, to be sure. And oysters, I believe?

RANK Yes, oysters; oysters, of course.

NORA And then all the port and champagne! It's sad that all these good things should attack the spine.

RANK Especially when the luckless spine attacked never had any good of them.

NORA Ah, yes, that's the worst of it.

RANK [*Looks at her searchingly.*] Hm...

NORA [*A moment later.*] Why did you smile?

RANK No, it was you that laughed.

NORA No, it was you that smiled, Doctor Rank.

RANK [*Standing up.*] I see you're deeper than I thought.

NORA I'm in such a crazy mood today.

RANK So it seems.

NORA [*With her hands on his shoulders.*] Dear, dear Doctor Rank, death shall not take you away from Torvald and me.

RANK Oh, you'll easily get over the loss. The absent are soon forgotten.

NORA [*Looks at him anxiously.*] Do you think so?

RANK People make fresh ties, and then...

NORA Who make fresh ties?

RANK You and Helmer will when I am gone. You yourself are taking time by the forelock, it seems to me. What was that Mrs Linden doing here yesterday?

NORA Oh!... you're surely not jealous of poor Christina?

RANK Yes, I am. She will be my successor in this house. When I am out of the way, this woman will perhaps...

NORA Hush! Not so loud! She's in there.

RANK Today as well? You see!

NORA Only to put my costume in order... dear me, how unreasonable you are! [*Sits on sofa.*] Now do be good, Doctor Rank! Tomorrow you shall see how beautifully I shall dance; and then you may fancy that I'm doing it all to please you... and, of course, Torvald as well. [*Takes various things out of box.*] Doctor Rank, sit down here, and I'll show you something.

RANK [*Sitting.*] What is it?

NORA Look here. Look!

RANK Silk stockings.

NORA Flesh-coloured. Aren't they lovely? It's so dark here now; but tomorrow... No, no, no, you must only look at the feet. Oh, well, I suppose you may look at the rest too.

RANK Hm...

NORA What are you looking so critical about? Do you think they won't fit me?

RANK I can't possibly give any competent opinion on that point.

NORA [*Looking at him a moment.*] For shame! [*Hits him lightly on the ear with the stockings.*] Take that. [*Rolls them up again.*]

RANK And what other wonders am I to see?

NORA You shan't see anything more, for you don't behave nicely.

[*She hums a little and searches among the things.*]

RANK [*After a short silence.*] When I sit here gossiping with you, I can't imagine… I simply cannot conceive… what would have become of me if I had never entered this house.

NORA [*Smiling.*] Yes, I think you do feel at home with us.

RANK [*More softly… looking straight before him.*] And now to have to leave it all…

NORA Nonsense. You shan't leave us.

RANK [*In the same tone.*] And not to be able to leave behind the slightest token of gratitude; scarcely even a passing regret… nothing but an empty place, that can be filled by the first comer.

NORA And if I were to ask you for…? No…

RANK For what?

NORA For a great proof of your friendship.

RANK Yes… yes?

NORA I mean… for a very, very great service…

RANK Would you really, for once, make me so happy?

NORA Oh, you don't know what it is.

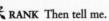

RANK Then tell me.

NORA No, I really can't, Doctor Rank. It's far, far too much... not only a service, but help and advice besides...

RANK So much the better. I can't think what you can mean. But go on. Don't you trust me?

NORA As I trust no one else. I know you are my best and truest friend. So I will tell you. Well then, Doctor Rank, there is something you must help me to prevent. You know how deeply, how wonderfully Torvald loves me; he wouldn't hesitate a moment to give his very life for my sake.

RANK [*Bending towards her.*] Nora... do you think he is the only one who...?

NORA [*With a slight start.*] Who...?

RANK Who would gladly give his life for you?

NORA [*Sadly.*] Oh!

RANK I have sworn that you shall know it before I... go. I shall never find a better opportunity. Yes, Nora, now I have told you; and now you know that you can trust me as you can no one else.

NORA [*Standing up; simply and calmly.*] Let me pass, please.

RANK [*Makes way for her, but remains sitting.*] Nora...

NORA [*In the doorway.*] Ellen, bring the lamp. [*Crosses to the stove.*] Oh dear, Doctor Rank, that was too bad of you.

RANK [*Rising.*] That I have loved you as deeply as... anyone else? Was that too bad of me?

NORA No, but that you should have told me so. It was so unnecessary...

RANK What do you mean? Did you know...?

[*ELLEN enters with the lamp; sets it on the table and goes out again.*]

RANK Nora... Mrs Helmer... I ask you, did you know?

NORA Oh, how can I tell what I knew or didn't know? I really can't say... How could you be so clumsy, Doctor Rank? It was all so nice!

RANK Well, at any rate, you know now that I am at your service, body and soul. And now, go on.

NORA [*Looking at him.*] Go on... now?

RANK I beg you to tell me what you want.

NORA I can tell you nothing now.

RANK Yes, yes! You mustn't punish me in that way. Let me do for you whatever a man can.

NORA You can do nothing for me now... Besides, I really want no help. You shall see it was only my fancy. Yes, it must be so. Of course! [*Sits in the rocking chair, looks at him and smiles.*] You are a nice person, Doctor Rank! Aren't you ashamed of yourself, now that the lamp is on the table?

RANK No, not exactly. But perhaps I ought to go… for ever.

NORA No, indeed you mustn't. Of course, you must come and go as you've always done. You know very well that Torvald can't do without you.

RANK Yes, but you?

NORA Oh, you know I always like to have you here.

RANK That is just what led me astray. You are a riddle to me. It has often seemed to me as if you liked being with me almost as much as being with Helmer.

NORA Yes, don't you see? There are people one loves, and others one likes to talk to.

RANK Yes… there's something in that.

NORA When I was a girl, of course I loved papa best. But it always delighted me to steal into the servants' room. In the first place they never lectured me, and in the second it was such fun to hear them talk.

RANK Ah, I see; then it's their place I have taken?

NORA [*Jumps up and hurries towards him.*] Oh, my dear Doctor Rank, I don't mean that. But you understand, with Torvald it's the same as with papa…

[*ELLEN enters from the hall.*]

ELLEN Please, ma'am… [*Whispers to NORA, and gives her a card.*]

NORA [*Glancing at card.*] Ah! [*Puts it in her pocket.*]

RANK Anything wrong?

NORA No, no, not in the least. It's only… it's my new costume…

RANK Your costume! Why, it's there.

NORA Oh, that one, yes. But this is another that… I have ordered it… Torvald mustn't know…

RANK Aha! So that's the great secret.

NORA Yes, of course. Please go to him; he's in the inner room. Do keep him while I…

RANK Don't be alarmed; he shan't escape.

[*RANK goes into HELMER's room.*]

NORA [*To ELLEN.*] Is he waiting in the kitchen?

ELLEN Yes, he came up the back stair…

NORA Didn't you tell him I was engaged?

ELLEN Yes, but it was no use.

NORA He won't go away?

ELLEN No, ma'am, not until he has spoken to you.

NORA Then let him come in; but quietly. And, Ellen… say nothing about it; it's a surprise for my husband.

ELLEN Oh, yes, ma'am, I understand.

[*She goes out.*]

NORA It is coming! The dreadful thing is coming, after all. No, no, no, it can never be; it shall not!

[*She goes to HELMER's door and slips the bolt. ELLEN opens the hall door for KROGSTAD, and shuts it after him. He wears a travelling coat, high boots, and a fur cap.*]

NORA [*Goes towards him.*] Speak softly; my husband is at home.

KROGSTAD All right. That's nothing to me.

NORA What do you want?

KROGSTAD A little information.

NORA Be quick, then. What is it?

KROGSTAD You know I have got my dismissal.

NORA I couldn't prevent it, Mr Krogstad. I fought for you to the last, but it was of no use.

KROGSTAD Does your husband care for you so little? He knows what I can bring upon you, and yet he dares...

NORA How could you think I should tell him?

KROGSTAD Well, as a matter of fact, I didn't think it. It wasn't like my friend Torvald Helmer to show so much courage...

NORA Mr Krogstad, be good enough to speak respectfully of my husband.

KROGSTAD Certainly, with all due respect. But since you are so anxious to keep the matter secret, I suppose you are a little clearer than yesterday as to what you have done.

NORA Clearer than you could ever make me.

KROGSTAD Yes, such a bad lawyer as I…

NORA What is it you want?

KROGSTAD Only to see how you are getting on, Mrs Helmer. I've been thinking about you all day. Even a mere money-lender, a gutter-journalist, a… in short, a creature like me… has a little bit of what people call feeling.

NORA Then show it; think of my little children.

KROGSTAD Did you and your husband think of mine? But enough of that. I only wanted to tell you that you needn't take this matter too seriously. I shall not lodge any information, for the present.

NORA No, surely not. I knew you wouldn't.

KROGSTAD The whole thing can be settled quite amicably. Nobody need know. It can remain among us three.

NORA My husband must never know.

KROGSTAD How can you prevent it? Can you pay off the balance?

NORA No, not at once.

KROGSTAD Or have you any means of raising the money in the next few days?

NORA None... that I will make use of.

KROGSTAD And if you had, it would not help you now. If you offered me ever so much money down, you should not get back your IOU.

NORA Tell me what you want to do with it.

KROGSTAD I only want to keep it... to have it in my possession. No outsider shall hear anything of it. So, if you have any desperate scheme in your head...

NORA What if I have?

KROGSTAD If you should think of leaving your husband and children...

NORA What if I do?

KROGSTAD Or if you should think of... something worse...

NORA How do you know that?

KROGSTAD Put all that out of your head.

NORA How did you know what I had in my mind?

KROGSTAD Most of us think of that at first. I thought of it, too, but I hadn't the courage...

NORA [*Tonelessly.*] Nor I.

KROGSTAD [*Relieved.*] No, one hasn't. You haven't the courage either, have you?

NORA I haven't, I haven't.

KROGSTAD Besides, it would be very foolish... Just one domestic storm, and it's all over. I have a letter in my pocket for your husband...

NORA Telling him everything?

KROGSTAD Sparing you as much as possible.

NORA [*Quickly.*] He must never read that letter. Tear it up. I will manage to get the money somehow...

KROGSTAD Pardon me, Mrs Helmer, but I believe I told you...

NORA Oh, I'm not talking about the money I owe you. Tell me how much you demand from my husband... I will get it.

KROGSTAD I demand no money from your husband.

NORA What do you demand then?

KROGSTAD I will tell you. I want to regain my footing in the world. I want to rise; and your husband shall help me to do it. For the last eighteen months my record has been spotless; I have been in bitter need all the time; but I was content to fight my way up, step by step. Now, I've been thrust down again, and I will not be satisfied with merely being reinstated as a matter of grace. I want to rise, I tell you. I must get into the Bank again, in a higher position than before. Your husband shall create a place on purpose for me...

NORA He will never do that!

KROGSTAD He will do it; I know him... he won't dare to show fight! And when he and I are together there, you shall soon see! Before a year is out I shall be the manager's right hand. It won't be Torvald Helmer, but Nils Krogstad, that manages the Joint Stock Bank.

NORA That shall never be.

KROGSTAD Perhaps you will...?

NORA Now I have the courage for it.

KROGSTAD Oh, you don't frighten me! A sensitive, petted creature like you...

NORA You shall see, you shall see!

KROGSTAD Under the ice, perhaps? Down into the cold, black water? And next spring to come up again, ugly, hairless, unrecognizable...

NORA You can't terrify me.

KROGSTAD Nor you me. People don't do that sort of thing, Mrs Helmer. And, after all, what would be the use of it? I have your husband in my pocket, all the same.

NORA Afterwards? When I am no longer...?

KROGSTAD You forget, your reputation remains in my hands! [*NORA stands speechless and looks at him.*] Well, now you are prepared. Do nothing foolish. As soon as Helmer has received my letter, I shall expect to hear from him. And remember that it is your husband himself who has forced me back again into such paths. That I will never forgive him. Goodbye, Mrs Helmer.

[*Goes out through the hall. NORA hurries to the door, opens it a little, and listens.*]

NORA He's going. He's not putting the letter into the box. No, no, it would be impossible! [*Opens the door further and further.*] What's that. He's standing still; not going downstairs. Has he changed his mind? Is he...? [*A letter falls into the box. KROGSTAD's footsteps are heard gradually receding down the stair. NORA utters a suppressed shriek, and rushes forward towards the sofa-table; pause.*] In the letter-box! [*Slips shrinkingly up to the hall door.*] There it lies... Torvald, Torvald... now we are lost!

[*Mrs LINDEN enters from the left with the costume.*]

Mrs LINDEN There, I think it's all right now. Shall we just try it on?

NORA [*Hoarsely and softly.*] Christina, come here.

Mrs LINDEN [*Throws down the dress on the sofa.*] What's the matter? You look quite distracted.

NORA Come here. Do you see that letter? There, see... through the glass of the letter-box.

Mrs LINDEN Yes, yes, I see it.

NORA That letter is from Krogstad...

Mrs LINDEN Nora... it was Krogstad who lent you the money?

NORA Yes, and now Torvald will know everything.

Mrs LINDEN Believe me, Nora, it's the best thing for both of you.

NORA You don't know all yet. I have forged a name...

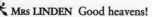

MRS LINDEN Good heavens!

NORA Now, listen to me, Christina; you shall bear me witness...

MRS LINDEN How "witness"? What am I to...?

NORA If I should go out of my mind... it might easily happen...

MRS LINDEN Nora!

NORA Or if anything else should happen to me... so that I couldn't be here...!

MRS LINDEN Nora, Nora, you're quite beside yourself!

NORA In case any one wanted to take it all upon himself... the whole blame... you understand...

MRS LINDEN Yes, yes; but how can you think...?

NORA You shall bear witness that it's not true, Christina. I'm not out of my mind at all; I know quite well what I'm saying; and I tell you nobody else knew anything about it; I did the whole thing, I myself. Remember that.

MRS LINDEN I shall remember. But I don't understand what you mean...

NORA Oh, how should you? It's the miracle coming to pass.

MRS LINDEN The miracle?

NORA Yes, the miracle. But it's so terrible, Christina; it mustn't happen for all the world.

MRS LINDEN I shall go straight to Krogstad and talk to him.

NORA Don't, he'll do you some harm.

MRS LINDEN Once he would have done anything for me.

NORA He?

MRS LINDEN Where does he live?

NORA Oh, how can I tell…? Yes… [*Feels in her pocket.*] Here's his card. But the letter, the letter…!

HELMER [*Knocking outside.*] Nora!

NORA [*Shrieks in terror.*] Oh, what is it? What do you want?

HELMER Well, well, don't be frightened. We're not coming in; you've bolted the door. Are you trying on your dress?

NORA Yes, yes, I'm trying it on. It suits me so well, Torvald.

MRS LINDEN [*Who has read the card.*] Why, he lives close by here.

NORA Yes, but it's no use now. We are lost. The letter is there in the box.

MRS LINDEN And your husband has the key?

NORA Always.

MRS LINDEN Krogstad must demand his letter back, unread. He must find some pretext…

NORA But this is the very time when Torvald generally…

MRS LINDEN Prevent him. Keep him occupied. I shall come back as quickly as I can.

[*She goes out hastily by the hall door.*]

NORA [*Opens HELMER's door and peeps in.*] Torvald!

HELMER Well, may one come into one's own room again at last? Come, Rank, we'll have a look... [*In the doorway.*] But how's this?

NORA What, Torvald dear?

HELMER Rank led me to expect a grand transformation.

RANK [*In the doorway.*] So I understood. I suppose I was mistaken.

NORA No, no one shall see me in my glory till tomorrow evening.

HELMER Why, Nora dear, you look so tired. Have you been practising too hard?

NORA No, I haven't practised at all yet.

HELMER But you'll have to...

NORA Oh yes, I must, I must! But, Torvald, I can't get on at all without your help. I've forgotten everything.

HELMER Oh, we shall soon freshen it up again.

NORA Yes, do help me, Torvald. You must promise me... Oh, I'm so nervous about it. Before so many people... This evening you must give yourself up entirely to me. You mustn't do a stroke of work; you mustn't even touch a pen. Do promise, Torvald dear!

HELMER I promise. All this evening I shall be your slave. Little helpless thing...! But, by the bye, I must just...

[*Going to hall door.*]

NORA What do you want there?

HELMER Only to see if there are any letters.

NORA No, no, don't do that, Torvald.

HELMER Why not?

NORA Torvald, I beg you not to. There are none there.

HELMER Let me just see. [*Heads off.*]

[*NORA, at the piano, plays the first bars of the tarantella.*]

HELMER [*At the door, stops.*] Aha!

NORA I can't dance tomorrow if I don't rehearse with you first.

HELMER [*Going to her.*] Are you really so nervous, dear Nora?

NORA Yes, dreadfully! Let me rehearse at once. We have time before dinner. Oh, do sit down and play for me, Torvald dear; direct me and put me right, as you used to do.

HELMER With all the pleasure in life, since you wish it. [*Sits at piano.*]

[*NORA snatches the tambourine out of the box, and hurriedly drapes herself in a long parti-coloured shawl; then, with a bound, stands in the middle of the floor.*]

NORA Now play for me! Now I'll dance!

[HELMER *plays and* NORA *dances.* RANK *stands at the piano behind* HELMER *and looks on.*]

HELMER [*Playing.*] Slower! Slower!

NORA Can't do it slower!

HELMER Not so violently, Nora.

NORA I must! I must!

HELMER [*Stops.*] No, no, Nora… that will never do.

NORA [*Laughs and swings her tambourine.*] Didn't I tell you so!

RANK Let me play for her.

HELMER [*Rising.*] Yes, do… then I can direct her better.

[RANK *sits down at the piano and plays;* NORA *dances more and more wildly.* HELMER *stands by the stove and addresses frequent corrections to her; she seems not to hear. Her hair breaks loose and falls over her shoulders. She does not notice it, but goes on dancing.* Mrs LINDEN *enters and stands spellbound in the doorway.*]

Mrs LINDEN Ah…!

NORA [*Dancing.*] We're having such fun here, Christina!

HELMER Why, Nora dear, you're dancing as if it were a matter of life and death.

NORA So it is.

HELMER Rank, stop! This is the merest madness. Stop, I say!

[*RANK stops playing and NORA comes to a sudden standstill.*]

HELMER [*Going towards her.*] I couldn't have believed it. You've positively forgotten all I taught you.

NORA [*Throws the tambourine away.*] You see for yourself.

HELMER You really do want teaching.

NORA Yes, you see how much I need it. You must practise with me up to the last moment. Will you promise me, Torvald?

HELMER Certainly, certainly.

NORA Neither today nor tomorrow must you think of anything but me. You mustn't open a single letter... mustn't look at the letter-box.

HELMER Ah, you're still afraid of that man...

NORA Oh yes, yes, I am.

HELMER Nora, I can see it in your face... there's a letter from him in the box.

NORA I don't know, I believe so. But you're not to read anything now; nothing ugly must come between us until everything is over.

RANK [*Softly, to HELMER.*] You mustn't contradict her.

HELMER [*Putting his arm around her.*] The child shall have her own way. But tomorrow night, when the dance is over...

NORA Then you shall be free.

[ELLEN *appears in the doorway, right.*]

ELLEN Dinner is on the table, ma'am.

NORA We'll have some champagne, Ellen.

ELLEN Yes, ma'am. [*Goes out.*]

HELMER Dear me! Quite a banquet.

NORA Yes, and we'll keep it up till morning. [*Calling out.*] And macaroons, Ellen… plenty… just this once.

HELMER [*Seizing her hand.*] Come, come, don't let us have this wild excitement! Be my own little lark again.

NORA Oh yes, I will. But now go into the dining room; and you too, Doctor Rank. Christina, you must help me to do up my hair.

RANK [*Softly, as they go.*] There's nothing in the wind? Nothing… I mean…?

HELMER Oh no, nothing of the kind. It's merely this babyish anxiety I was telling you about.

[*They go out to the right.*]

NORA Well?

Mrs LINDEN He's gone out of town.

NORA I saw it in your face.

Mrs LINDEN He comes back tomorrow evening. I left a note for him.

NORA You shouldn't have done that. Things must take their course. After all, there's something glorious in waiting for the miracle.

Mrs LINDEN What is it you're waiting for?

NORA Oh, you can't understand. Go to them in the dining room; I shall come in a moment.

[*Mrs LINDEN goes into the dining room. NORA stands for a moment as though collecting her thoughts; then looks at her watch.*]

NORA Seven hours till midnight. Then twenty-four hours till the next midnight. Then the tarantella will be over. Twenty-four and seven? Thirty-one hours to live.

[*HELMER appears at the door, right.*]

HELMER What has become of my little lark?

NORA [*Runs to him with open arms.*] Here she is!

ACT THIRD

The same room. The table, with the chairs around it, in the middle. A lamp lit on the table. The door to the hall stands open. Dance music is heard from the floor above.

MRS LINDEN sits by the table and absently turns the pages of a book. She tries to read, but seems unable to fix her attention; she frequently listens and looks anxiously towards the hall door.

MRS LINDEN [*Looks at her watch.*] Not here yet; and the time is nearly up. If only he hasn't… [*Listens again.*] Ah, there he is. [*She goes into the hall and cautiously opens the outer door; soft footsteps are heard on the stairs; she whispers.*] Come in; there is no one here.

KROGSTAD [*In the doorway.*] I found a note from you at my house. What does it mean?

MRS LINDEN I must speak to you.

KROGSTAD Indeed? And in this house?

MRS LINDEN I could not see you at my rooms. They have no separate entrance. Come in; we are quite alone. The servants are asleep, and the Helmers are at the ball upstairs.

KROGSTAD [*Coming into the room.*] Ah! So the Helmers are dancing this evening? Really?

MRS LINDEN Yes. Why not?

KROGSTAD Quite right. Why not?

Mrs LINDEN And now let us talk a little.

KROGSTAD Have we two anything to say to each other?

Mrs LINDEN A great deal.

KROGSTAD I should not have thought so.

Mrs LINDEN Because you have never really understood me.

KROGSTAD What was there to understand? The most natural thing in the world… a heartless woman throws a man over when a better match offers.

Mrs LINDEN Do you really think me so heartless? Do you think I broke with you lightly?

KROGSTAD Did you not?

Mrs LINDEN Do you really think so?

KROGSTAD If not, why did you write me that letter?

Mrs LINDEN Was it not best? Since I had to break with you, was it not right that I should try to put an end to all that you felt for me?

KROGSTAD [*Clenching his hands together.*] So that was it? And all this… for the sake of money!

Mrs LINDEN You ought not to forget that I had a helpless mother and two little brothers. We could not wait for you, Nils, as your prospects then stood.

KROGSTAD Perhaps not; but you had no right to cast me off for the sake of others, whoever the others might be.

Mrs LINDEN I don't know. I have often asked myself whether I had the right.

KROGSTAD [*More softly.*] When I had lost you, I seemed to have no firm ground left under my feet. Look at me now. I am a shipwrecked man clinging to a spar.

Mrs LINDEN Rescue may be at hand.

KROGSTAD It was at hand; but then you came and stood in the way.

Mrs LINDEN Without my knowledge, Nils. I did not know till today that it was you I was to replace in the Bank.

KROGSTAD Well, I take your word for it. But now that you do know, do you mean to give way?

Mrs LINDEN No, for that would not help you in the least.

KROGSTAD Oh, help, help…! I should do it whether or no.

Mrs LINDEN I have learnt prudence. Life and bitter necessity have schooled me.

KROGSTAD And life has taught me not to trust fine speeches.

Mrs LINDEN Then life has taught you a very sensible thing. But deeds you will trust?

KROGSTAD What do you mean?

MRS LINDEN You said you were a shipwrecked man, clinging to a spar.

KROGSTAD I have good reason to say so.

MRS LINDEN I too am shipwrecked, and clinging to a spar. I have no one to mourn for, no one to care for.

KROGSTAD You made your own choice.

MRS LINDEN No choice was left me.

KROGSTAD Well, what then?

MRS LINDEN Nils, how if we two shipwrecked people could join hands?

KROGSTAD What!

MRS LINDEN Two on a raft have a better chance than if each clings to a separate spar.

KROGSTAD Christina!

MRS LINDEN What do you think brought me to town?

KROGSTAD Had you any thought of me?

MRS LINDEN I must have work or I can't bear to live. All my life, as long as I can remember, I have worked; work has been my one great joy. Now I stand quite alone in the world, aimless and forlorn. There is no happiness in working for one's self. Nils, give me somebody and something to work for.

KROGSTAD I cannot believe in all this. It is simply a woman's romantic craving for self-sacrifice.

MRS LINDEN Have you ever found me romantic?

KROGSTAD Would you really...? Tell me: do you know all my past?

MRS LINDEN Yes.

KROGSTAD And do you know what people say of me?

MRS LINDEN Did you not say just now that with me you could
have been another man?

KROGSTAD I am sure of it.

MRS LINDEN Is it too late?

KROGSTAD Christina, do you know what you are doing? Yes, you
do; I see it in your face. Have you the courage then...?

MRS LINDEN I need someone to be a mother to, and your children
need a mother. You need me, and I... I need you. Nils, I believe in
your better self. With you I fear nothing.

KROGSTAD [*Seizing her hands.*] Thank you... thank you, Christina.
Now I shall make others see me as you do. Ah, I forgot...

MRS LINDEN [*Listening.*] Hush! The tarantella! Go! go!

KROGSTAD Why? What is it?

MRS LINDEN Don't you hear the dancing overhead? As soon as that
is over they will be here.

KROGSTAD Oh yes, I shall go. Nothing will come of this, after
all. Of course, you don't know the step I have taken against
the Helmers.

Mrs LINDEN Yes, Nils, I do know.

KROGSTAD And yet you have the courage to…?

Mrs LINDEN I know to what lengths despair can drive a man.

KROGSTAD Oh, if I could only undo it!

Mrs LINDEN You could. Your letter is still in the box.

KROGSTAD Are you sure?

Mrs LINDEN Yes; but…

KROGSTAD [*Looking to her searchingly.*] Is that what it all means? You want to save your friend at any price. Say it out… is that your idea?

Mrs LINDEN Nils, a woman who has once sold herself for the sake of others, does not do so again.

KROGSTAD I shall demand my letter back again.

Mrs LINDEN No, no.

KROGSTAD Yes, of course. I shall wait till Helmer comes; I shall tell him to give it back to me… that it's only about my dismissal… that I don't want it read…

Mrs LINDEN No, Nils, you must not recall the letter.

KROGSTAD But tell me, wasn't that just why you got me to come here?

Mrs LINDEN Yes, in my first alarm. But a day has passed since then, and in that day I have seen incredible things in this house. Helmer must know everything; there must be an end to this unhappy secret. These two must come to a full understanding. They must have done with all these shifts and subterfuges.

KROGSTAD Very well, if you like to risk it. But one thing I can do, and at once…

Mrs LINDEN [*Listening.*] Make haste! Go, go! The dance is over; we're not safe another moment.

KROGSTAD I shall wait for you in the street.

Mrs LINDEN Yes, do; you must see me home.

KROGSTAD I never was so happy in all my life!

[*KROGSTAD goes out by the outer door. The door between the room and the hall remains open.*]

Mrs LINDEN [*Arranging the room and getting her outdoor things together.*] What a change! What a change! To have someone to work for, to live for; a home to make happy! Well, it shall not be my fault if I fail. I wish they would come… [*Listens.*] Ah, here they are! I must get my things on.

[*Takes bonnet and cloak. HELMER's and NORA's voices are heard outside, a key is turned in the lock, and HELMER drags NORA almost by force into the hall. She wears the Italian costume with a large black shawl over it. He is in evening dress and wears a black domino, open.*]

NORA [*Struggling with him in the doorway.*] No, no, no! I won't go in! I want to go upstairs again; I don't want to leave so early!

HELMER But, my dearest girl…!

NORA Oh, please, please, Torvald, I beseech you… only one hour more!

HELMER Not one minute more, Nora dear; you know what we agreed. Come, come in; you're catching cold here. [*He leads her gently into the room in spite of her resistance.*]

Mrs LINDEN Good evening.

NORA Christina!

HELMER What, Mrs Linden! You here so late?

Mrs LINDEN Yes, I ought to apologize. I did so want to see Nora in her costume.

NORA Have you been sitting here waiting for me?

Mrs LINDEN Yes; unfortunately I came too late. You had gone upstairs already, and I felt I couldn't go away without seeing you.

HELMER [*Taking Nora's shawl off.*] Well then, just look at her! I assure you she's worth it. Isn't she lovely, Mrs Linden?

Mrs LINDEN Yes, I must say…

HELMER Isn't she exquisite? Everyone said so. But she's dreadfully obstinate, dear little creature. What's to be done with her? Just think, I had almost to force her away.

NORA Oh, Torvald, you'll be sorry some day that you didn't let me stay, if only for one half-hour more.

HELMER There! You hear her, Mrs Linden? She dances her tarantella with wild applause, and well she deserved it, I must say... though there was, perhaps, a little too much nature in her rendering of the idea... more than was, strictly speaking, artistic. But never mind... the point is, she made a great success, a tremendous success. Was I to let her remain after that... to weaken the impression? Not if I know it. I took my sweet little Capri girl... my capricious little Capri girl, I might say... under my arm; a rapid turn round the room, a curtsey to all sides, and... as they say in novels... the lovely apparition vanished! An exit should always be effective, Mrs Linden; but I can't get Nora to see it. By Jove! it's warm here. [*Throws his domino on a chair and opens the door to his room.*] What! No light there? Oh, of course. Excuse me...

[*Goes in and lights candle.*]

NORA [*Whispers breathlessly.*] Well?

MRS LINDEN [*Softly.*] I've spoken to him.

NORA And...?

MRS LINDEN Nora... you must tell your husband everything...

NORA [*Tonelessly.*] I knew it!

MRS LINDEN You have nothing to fear from Krogstad; but you must speak out.

NORA I shall not speak!

MRS LINDEN Then the letter will.

NORA Thank you, Christina. Now I know what I have to do. Hush...!

HELMER [*Coming back.*] Well, Mrs Linden, have you admired her?

Mrs LINDEN Yes, and now I must say goodnight.

HELMER What, already? Does this knitting belong to you?

Mrs LINDEN [*Takes it.*] Yes, thanks; I was nearly forgetting it.

HELMER Then you do knit?

Mrs LINDEN Yes.

HELMER Do you know, you ought to embroider instead?

Mrs LINDEN Indeed! Why?

HELMER Because it's so much prettier. Look now! You hold the embroidery in the left hand, so, and then work the needle with the right hand, in a long, graceful curve... don't you?

Mrs LINDEN Yes, I suppose so.

HELMER But knitting is always ugly. Just look... your arms close to your sides, and the needles going up and down... there's something Chinese about it... They really gave us splendid champagne tonight.

Mrs LINDEN Well, goodnight, Nora, and don't be obstinate any more.

HELMER Well said, Mrs Linden!

Mrs LINDEN Goodnight, Mr Helmer.

HELMER [*Accompanying her to the door.*] Goodnight, goodnight; I hope you'll get safely home. I should be glad to... but you have such a short way to go. Goodnight, goodnight. [*She goes; HELMER shuts the door after her and comes forward again.*] At last we've got rid of her: she's a terrible bore.

NORA Aren't you very tired, Torvald?

HELMER No, not in the least.

NORA Nor sleepy?

HELMER Not a bit. I feel particularly lively. But you? You do look tired and sleepy.

NORA Yes, very tired. I shall soon sleep now.

HELMER There, you see. I was right after all not to let you stay longer.

NORA Oh, everything you do is right.

HELMER [*Kissing her forehead.*] Now my lark is speaking like a reasonable being. Did you notice how jolly Rank was this evening?

NORA Indeed? Was he? I had no chance of speaking to him.

HELMER Nor I, much; but I haven't seen him in such good spirits for a long time. [*Looks at NORA a little, then comes nearer her.*] It's splendid to be back in our own home, to be quite alone together! Oh, you enchanting creature!

NORA Don't look at me in that way, Torvald.

HELMER I am not to look at my dearest treasure?… at all the loveliness that is mine, mine only, wholly and entirely mine?

NORA [*Goes to the other side of the table.*] You mustn't say these things to me this evening.

HELMER [*Following.*] I see you have the tarantella still in your blood... and that makes you all the more enticing. Listen! The other people are going now. [*More softly.*] Nora... soon the whole house will be still.

NORA Yes, I hope so.

HELMER Yes, don't you, Nora darling? When we are among strangers, do you know why I speak so little to you, and keep so far away, and only steal a glance at you now and then... do you know why I do it? Because I am fancying that we love each other in secret, that I am secretly betrothed to you, and that no one dreams that there is anything between us.

NORA Yes, yes, yes. I know all your thoughts are with me.

HELMER And then, when the time comes to go, and I put the shawl about your smooth, soft shoulders, and this glorious neck of yours, I imagine you are my bride, that our marriage is just over, that I am bringing you for the first time to my home... that I am alone with you for the first time... quite alone with you, in your trembling loveliness! All this evening I have been longing for you, and you only. When I watched you swaying and whirling in the tarantella... my blood boiled... I could endure it no longer; and that's why I made you come home with me so early...

NORA Go now, Torvald! Go away from me. I won't have all this.

HELMER What do you mean? Ah, I see you're teasing me, little Nora! Won't... won't! Am I not your husband...?

[*A knock at the outer door.*]

NORA [*Starts.*] Did you hear...?

HELMER [*Going towards the hall.*] Who's there?

RANK [*Outside.*] It is I; may I come in for a moment?

HELMER [*In a low tone, annoyed.*] Oh, what can he want just now?
[*Aloud.*] Wait a moment. [*Opens door.*] Come, it's nice of you to
look in.

RANK I thought I heard your voice, and that put it into my head.
[*Looks round.*] Ah, this dear old place! How cosy you two are here!

HELMER You seemed to find it pleasant enough upstairs, too.

RANK Exceedingly. Why not? Why shouldn't one take one's share
of everything in this world? All one can, at least, and as long as one
can. The wine was splendid...

HELMER Especially the champagne.

RANK Did you notice it? It's incredible the quantity I contrived to
get down.

NORA Torvald drank plenty of champagne, too.

RANK Did he?

NORA Yes, and it always puts him in such spirits.

RANK Well, why shouldn't one have a jolly evening after a well-
spent day?

HELMER Well-spent! Well, I haven't much to boast of in that
respect.

RANK [*Slapping him on the shoulder.*] But I have, don't you see?

NORA I suppose you have been engaged in a scientific investigation, Doctor Rank?

RANK Quite right.

HELMER Bless me! Little Nora talking about scientific investigations!

NORA Am I to congratulate you on the result?

RANK By all means.

NORA It was good then?

RANK The best possible, both for doctor and patient... certainty.

NORA [*Quickly and searchingly.*] Certainty?

RANK Absolute certainty. Wasn't I right to enjoy myself after that?

NORA Yes, quite right, Doctor Rank.

HELMER And so say I, provided you don't have to pay for it tomorrow.

RANK Well, in this life nothing is to be had for nothing.

NORA Doctor Rank... I'm sure you are very fond of masquerades?

RANK Yes, when there are plenty of amusing disguises...

NORA Tell me, what shall we two be at our next masquerade?

HELMER Little featherbrain! Thinking of your next already!

RANK We two? I'll tell you. You must go as a good fairy.

HELMER Ah, but what costume would indicate that?

RANK She has simply to wear her everyday dress.

HELMER Capital! But don't you know what you will be yourself?

RANK Yes, my dear friend, I am perfectly clear upon that point.

HELMER Well?

RANK At the next masquerade I shall be invisible.

HELMER What a comical idea!

RANK There's a big black hat... haven't you heard of the invisible hat? It comes down all over you, and then no one can see you.

HELMER [*With a suppressed smile.*] No, you're right there.

RANK But I'm quite forgetting what I came for. Helmer, give me a cigar... one of the dark Havanas.

HELMER With the greatest pleasure.

[*Hands cigar case.*]

RANK [*Takes one and cuts the end off.*] Thank you.

NORA [*Striking a wax match.*] Let me give you a light.

RANK A thousand thanks.

[*She holds the match. He lights his cigar with it.*]

RANK And now, goodbye!

HELMER Goodbye, goodbye, my dear fellow.

NORA Sleep well, Doctor Rank.

RANK Thanks for the wish.

NORA Wish me the same.

RANK You? Very well, since you ask me... Sleep well. And thanks for the light.

[*He nods to them both and goes out.*]

HELMER [*In an undertone.*] He's been drinking a good deal.

NORA [*Absently.*] I dare say. [*HELMER takes his bunch of keys from his pocket and goes into the hall.*] Torvald, what are you doing there?

HELMER I must empty the letter-box; it's quite full; there will be no room for the newspapers tomorrow morning.

NORA Are you going to work tonight?

HELMER You know very well I am not... Why, how is this? Some one has been at the lock.

NORA The lock...?

HELMER I'm sure of it. What does it mean? I can't think that the servants...? Here's a broken hair-pin. Nora, it's one of yours.

NORA [*Quickly.*] It must have been the children...

HELMER Then you must break them of such tricks... There! At last I've got it open. [*Takes contents out and calls into the kitchen.*] Ellen!... Ellen, just put the hall door lamp out.

[*He returns with letters in his hand, and shuts the inner door.*]

HELMER Just see how they've accumulated. [*Turning them over.*] Why, what's this?

NORA [*At the window.*] The letter! Oh no, no, Torvald!

HELMER Two visiting cards... from Rank.

NORA From Doctor Rank?

HELMER [*Looking at them.*] Doctor Rank. They were on the top. He must just have put them in.

NORA Is there anything on them?

HELMER There's a black cross over the name. Look at it. What an unpleasant idea! It looks just as if he were announcing his own death.

NORA So he is.

HELMER What! Do you know anything? Has he told you anything?

NORA Yes. These cards mean that he has taken his last leave of us. He is going to shut himself up and die.

HELMER Poor fellow! Of course, I knew we couldn't hope to keep

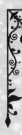

him long. But so soon…! And to go and creep into his lair like a wounded animal…

NORA When we must go, it is best to go silently. Don't you think so, Torvald?

HELMER [*Walking up and down.*] He had so grown into our lives, I can't realize that he is gone. He and his sufferings and his loneliness formed a sort of cloudy background to the sunshine of our happiness… Well, perhaps it's best as it is… at any rate for him. [*Stands still.*] And perhaps for us too, Nora. Now we two are thrown entirely upon each other. [*Takes her in his arms.*] My darling wife! I feel as if I could never hold you close enough. Do you know, Nora, I often wish some danger might threaten you, that I might risk body and soul, and everything, everything, for your dear sake.

NORA [*Tears herself from him and says firmly.*] Now you shall read your letters, Torvald.

HELMER No, no; not tonight. I want to be with you, my sweet wife.

NORA With the thought of your dying friend…?

HELMER You are right. This has shaken us both. Unloveliness has come between us… thoughts of death and decay. We must seek to cast them off. Till then… we will remain apart.

NORA [*Her arms round his neck.*] Torvald! Goodnight! Goodnight!

HELMER [*Kissing her forehead.*] Goodnight, my little song bird. Sleep well, Nora. Now I shall go and read my letters.

[*He goes with the letters in his hand into his room and shuts the door.*]

NORA [*With wild eyes, gropes about her, seizes HELMER's domino, throws it round her, and whispers quickly, hoarsely, and brokenly.*] Never to see him again. Never, never, never. [*Throws her shawl over her head.*] Never to see the children again. Never, never... Oh that black, icy water! Oh that bottomless...! If it were only over! Now he has it; he's reading it. Oh, no, no, no, not yet. Torvald, goodbye...! Goodbye, my little ones...!

[*She is rushing out by the hall; at the same moment HELMER flings his door open, and stands there with an open letter in his hand.*]

HELMER Nora!

NORA [*Shrieks.*] Ah...!

HELMER What is this? Do you know what is in this letter?

NORA Yes, I know. Let me go! Let me pass!

HELMER [*Holds her back.*] Where do you want to go?

NORA [*Tries to break away from him.*] You shall not save me, Torvald.

HELMER [*Falling back.*] True! Is what he writes true? No, no, it is impossible that this can be true.

NORA It is true. I have loved you beyond all else in the world.

HELMER Pshaw... no silly evasions!

NORA [*A step nearer him.*] Torvald...!

HELMER Wretched woman... what have you done!

NORA Let me go... you shall not save me! You shall not take my guilt upon yourself!

HELMER I don't want any melodramatic airs. [*Locks the outer door.*] Here you shall stay and give an account of yourself. Do you understand what you have done? Answer! Do you understand it?

NORA [*Looks at him fixedly, and says with a stiffening expression.*] Yes, now I begin fully to understand it.

HELMER [*Walking up and down.*] Oh! what an awful awakening! During all these eight years... she who was my pride and my joy... a hypocrite, a liar... worse, worse... a criminal. Oh, the unfathomable hideousness of it all! Ugh! Ugh!

[*NORA says nothing, and continues to look fixedly at him.*]

HELMER I ought to have known how it would be. I ought to have foreseen it. All your father's want of principle... be silent!... all your father's want of principle you have inherited... no religion, no morality, no sense of duty. How I am punished for screening him! I did it for your sake; and you reward me like this.

NORA Yes... like this.

HELMER You have destroyed my whole happiness. You have ruined my future. Oh, it's frightful to think of! I am in the power of a scoundrel; he can do whatever he pleases with me, demand whatever he chooses; he can domineer over me as much as he likes, and I must submit. And all this disaster and ruin is brought upon me by an unprincipled woman!

NORA When I am out of the world, you will be free.

HELMER Oh, no fine phrases. Your father, too, was always ready with them. What good would it do me, if you were "out of the world", as you say? No good whatever! He can publish the story all the same; I might even be suspected of collusion. People will think I was at the bottom of it all and egged you on. And for all this I have you to thank... you whom I have done nothing but pet and spoil during our whole married life. Do you understand now what you have done to me?

NORA [*With cold calmness.*] Yes.

HELMER The thing is so incredible, I can't grasp it. But we must come to an understanding. Take that shawl off. Take it off, I say! I must try to pacify him in one way or another... the matter must be hushed up, cost what it may... As for you and me, we must make no outward change in our way of life... no outward change, you understand. Of course, you will continue to live here. But the children cannot be left in your care. I dare not trust them to you... Oh, to have to say this to one I have loved so tenderly... whom I still...! But that must be a thing of the past. Henceforward there can be no question of happiness, but merely of saving the ruins, the shreds, the show... [*A ring; HELMER starts.*] What's that? So late! Can it be the worst? Can he...? Hide yourself, Nora; say you are ill.

[*NORA stands motionless. HELMER goes to the door and opens it.*]

ELLEN [*Half dressed, in the hall.*] Here is a letter for you, ma'am.

HELMER Give it to me. [*Seizes the letter and shuts the door.*] Yes, from him. You shall not have it. I shall read it.

NORA Read it?

HELMER [*By the lamp.*] I have hardly the courage to. We may both be lost, both you and I. Ah! I must know. [*Hastily tears the letter open; reads a few lines, looks at an enclosure; with a cry of joy.*] Nora!

[*Nora looks inquiringly at him.*]

HELMER Nora!... Oh! I must read it again... Yes, yes, it is so. I am saved! Nora, I am saved!

NORA And I?

HELMER You too, of course; we are both saved, both of us. Look here... he sends you back your promissory note. He writes that he regrets and apologizes, that a happy turn in his life... Oh, what matter what he writes. We are saved, Nora! No one can harm you. Oh, Nora, Nora..., but first to get rid of this hateful thing. I'll just see... [*Glances at the IOU.*] No, I will not look at it; the whole thing shall be nothing but a dream to me. [*Tears the IOU and both letters in pieces. Throws them into the fire and watches them burn.*] There! It's gone!... He said that ever since Christmas Eve... Oh, Nora, they must have been three terrible days for you!

NORA I have fought a hard fight for the last three days.

HELMER And in your agony you saw no other outlet but... No, we won't think of that horror. We will only rejoice and repeat... it's over, all over! Don't you hear, Nora? You don't seem able to grasp it. Yes, it's over. What is this set look on your face? Oh, my poor Nora, I understand; you cannot believe that I have forgiven you. But I have, Nora; I swear it. I have forgiven everything. I know that what you did was all for love of me.

NORA That is true.

HELMER You loved me as a wife should love her husband. It was only the means that, in your inexperience, you misjudged. But do you think I love you the less because you cannot do without guidance? No, no. Only lean on me; I will counsel you, and guide you. I should be no true man if this very womanly helplessness did not make you doubly dear in my eyes. You mustn't dwell upon the hard things I said in my first moment of terror, when the world seemed to be tumbling about my ears. I have forgiven you, Nora... I swear I have forgiven you.

NORA I thank you for your forgiveness.

[*Goes out, to the right.*]

HELMER No, stay...! [*Looking through the doorway.*] What are you going to do?

NORA [*Inside.*] To take off my masquerade dress.

HELMER [*In the doorway.*] Yes, do, dear. Try to calm down, and recover your balance, my scared little song bird. You may rest secure. I have broad wings to shield you. [*Walking up and down near the door.*] Oh, how lovely... how cosy our home is, Nora! Here you are safe; here I can shelter you like a hunted dove whom I have saved from the claws of the hawk. I shall soon bring your poor beating heart to rest; believe me, Nora, very soon. Tomorrow all this will seem quite different... everything will be as before. I shall not need to tell you again that I forgive you; you will feel for yourself that it is true. How could you think I could find it in my heart to drive you away, or even so much as to reproach you? Oh, you don't know a true man's heart, Nora. There is something indescribably sweet and soothing to a man in having forgiven his wife... honestly forgiven her, from the bottom of his heart. She becomes his property in a double sense. She is as though born again; she has become, so to speak, at once his wife and his child. That is what you shall henceforth be to me, my bewildered, helpless darling.

Don't be troubled about anything, Nora; only open your heart to me, and I will be both will and conscience to you. [*NORA enters in everyday dress.*] Why, what's this? Not gone to bed. You have changed your dress?

NORA Yes, Torvald; now I have changed my dress.

HELMER But why now, so late...?

NORA I shall not sleep tonight.

HELMER But, Nora dear...

NORA [*Looking at her watch.*] It's not so late yet. Sit down, Torvald; you and I have much to say to each other.

[*She sits at one side of the table.*]

HELMER Nora... what does this mean? Your cold, set face...

NORA Sit down. It will take some time. I have much to talk over with you.

[*HELMER sits at the other side of the table.*]

HELMER You alarm me, Nora; I don't understand you.

NORA No, that is just it. You don't understand me; and I have never understood you... till tonight. No, don't interrupt. Only listen to what I say... We must come to a final settlement, Torvald.

HELMER How do you mean?

NORA [*After a short silence.*] Does not one thing strike you as we sit here?

HELMER What should strike me?

NORA We have been married eight years. Does it not strike you that this is the first time we two, you and I, man and wife, have talked together seriously?

HELMER Seriously! What do you call seriously?

NORA During eight whole years, and more... ever since the day we first met... we have never exchanged one serious word about serious things.

HELMER Was I always to trouble you with the cares you could not help me to bear?

NORA I am not talking of cares. I say that we have never yet set ourselves seriously to get to the bottom of anything.

HELMER Why, my dearest Nora, what have you to do with serious things?

NORA There we have it! You have never understood me... I have had great injustice done me, Torvald; first by father, and then by you.

HELMER What! By your father and me?... By us, who have loved you more than all the world?

NORA [*Shaking her head.*] You have never loved me. You only thought it amusing to be in love with me.

HELMER Why, Nora, what a thing to say!

NORA Yes, it is so, Torvald. While I was at home with father, he used to tell me all his opinions, and I held the same opinions. If

I had others I said nothing about them, because he wouldn't have liked it. He used to call me his doll-child, and played with me as I played with my dolls. Then I came to live in your house…

HELMER What an expression to use about our marriage!

NORA [*Undisturbed.*] I mean I passed from father's hands into yours. You arranged everything according to your taste; and I got the same tastes as you; or I pretended to… I don't know which… both ways, perhaps; sometimes one and sometimes the other. When I look back on it now, I seem to have been living here like a beggar, from hand to mouth. I lived by performing tricks for you, Torvald. But you would have it so. You and father have done me a great wrong. It is your fault that my life has come to nothing.

HELMER Why, Nora, how unreasonable and ungrateful you are! Have you not been happy here?

NORA No, never. I thought I was; but I never was.

HELMER Not… not happy!

NORA No, only merry. And you have always been so kind to me. But our house has been nothing but a play-room. Here I have been your doll-wife, just as at home I used to be papa's doll-child. And the children, in their turn, have been my dolls. I thought it fun when you played with me, just as the children did when I played with them. That has been our marriage, Torvald.

HELMER There is some truth in what you say, exaggerated and overstrained though it be. But henceforth it shall be different. Play-time is over; now comes the time for education.

NORA Whose education? Mine, or the children's?

HELMER Both, my dear Nora.

NORA Oh, Torvald, you are not the man to teach me to be a fit wife for you.

HELMER And you can say that?

NORA And I... how have I prepared myself to educate the children?

HELMER Nora!

NORA Did you not say yourself, a few minutes ago, you dared not trust them to me?

HELMER In the excitement of the moment! Why should you dwell upon that?

NORA No... you were perfectly right. That problem is beyond me. There is another to be solved first... I must try to educate myself. You are not the man to help me in that. I must set about it alone. And that is why I am leaving you.

HELMER [*Jumping up.*] What do you mean to say...?

NORA I must stand quite alone if I am ever to know myself and my surroundings, so I cannot stay with you.

HELMER Nora! Nora!

NORA I am going at once. I dare say Christina will take me in for tonight...

HELMER You are mad! I shall not allow it! I forbid it!

NORA It is of no use your forbidding me anything now. I shall take with me what belongs to me. From you I will accept nothing, either now or afterwards.

HELMER What madness this is!

NORA Tomorrow I shall go home... I mean to what was my home. It will be easier for me to find some opening there.

HELMER Oh, in your blind inexperience...

NORA I must try to gain experience, Torvald.

HELMER To forsake your home, your husband, and your children! And you don't consider what the world will say.

NORA I can pay no heed to that. I only know that I must do it.

HELMER This is monstrous! Can you forsake your holiest duties in this way?

NORA What do you consider my holiest duties?

HELMER Do I need to tell you that? Your duties to your husband and your children.

NORA I have other duties equally sacred.

HELMER Impossible! What duties do you mean?

NORA My duties towards myself.

HELMER Before all else you are a wife and a mother.

NORA That I no longer believe. I believe that before all else I am a human being, just as much as you are... or at least that I should try to become one. I know that most people agree with you, Torvald, and that they say so in books. But henceforth I can't be satisfied with what most people say, and what is in books. I must think things out for myself, and try to get clear about them.

HELMER Are you not clear about your place in your own home? Have you not an infallible guide in questions like these? Have you not religion?

NORA Oh, Torvald, I don't really know what religion is.

HELMER What do you mean?

NORA I know nothing but what Pastor Hansen told me when I was confirmed. He explained that religion was this and that. When I get away from all this and stand alone, I will look into that matter too. I will see whether what he taught me is right, or, at any rate, whether it is right for me.

HELMER Oh, this is unheard of! And from so young a woman! But if religion cannot keep you right, let me appeal to your conscience… for I suppose you have some moral feeling? Or, answer me: perhaps you have none?

NORA Well, Torvald, it's not easy to say. I really don't know… I am all at sea about these things. I only know that I think quite differently from you about them. I hear, too, that the laws are different from what I thought: but I can't believe that they can be right. It appears that a woman has no right to spare her dying father, or to save her husband's life! I don't believe that.

HELMER You talk like a child. You don't understand the society in which you live.

NORA No, I do not. But now I shall try to learn. I must make up my mind which is right… society or I.

HELMER Nora, you are ill; you are feverish; I almost think you are out of your senses.

NORA I have never felt so much clearness and certainty as tonight.

HELMER You are clear and certain enough to forsake husband and children?

NORA Yes, I am.

HELMER Then there is only one explanation possible.

NORA What is that?

HELMER You no longer love me.

NORA No, that is just it.

HELMER Nora!… Can you say so!

NORA Oh, I'm so sorry, Torvald; for you've always been so kind to me. But I can't help it. I do not love you any longer.

HELMER [*Mastering himself with difficulty.*] Are you clear and certain on this point too?

NORA Yes, quite. That is why I will not stay here any longer.

HELMER And can you also make clear to me how I have forfeited your love?

NORA Yes, I can. It was this evening, when the miracle did not happen; for then I saw you were not the man I had imagined.

HELMER Explain yourself more clearly; I don't understand.

NORA I have waited so patiently all these eight years, for of course I saw clearly enough that miracles don't happen every day. When this crushing blow threatened me, I said to myself so confidently, "Now comes the miracle!" When Krogstad's letter lay in the box, it never for a moment occurred to me that you would think of submitting to that man's conditions. I was convinced that you would say to him, "Make it known to all the world"; and that then…

HELMER Well? When I had given my own wife's name up to disgrace and shame…?

NORA Then I firmly believed that you would come forward, take everything upon yourself, and say, "I am the guilty one."

HELMER Nora…!

NORA You mean I would never have accepted such a sacrifice? No, certainly not. But what would my assertions have been worth in opposition to yours?… That was the miracle that I hoped for and dreaded. And it was to hinder that that I wanted to die.

HELMER I would gladly work for you day and night, Nora… bear sorrow and want for your sake. But no man sacrifices his honour, even for one he loves.

NORA Millions of women have done so.

HELMER Oh, you think and talk like a silly child.

NORA Very likely. But you neither think nor talk like the man I can share my life with. When your terror was over... not for what threatened me, but for yourself... when there was nothing more to fear... then it seemed to you as though nothing had happened. I was your lark again, your doll, just as before... whom you would take twice as much care of in future, because she was so weak and fragile. [*Stands up.*] Torvald... in that moment it burst upon me that I had been living here these eight years with a strange man, and had borne him three children... Oh, I can't bear to think of it! I could tear myself to pieces!

HELMER [*Sadly.*] I see it, I see it; an abyss has opened between us... But, Nora, can it never be filled up?

NORA As I now am, I am no wife for you.

HELMER I have strength to become another man.

NORA Perhaps... when your doll is taken away from you.

HELMER To part... to part from you! No, Nora, no; I can't grasp the thought.

NORA [*Going into room on the right.*] The more reason for the thing to happen.

[*She comes back with outdoor things and a small travelling bag, which she places on a chair.*]

HELMER Nora, Nora, not now! Wait till tomorrow.

NORA [*Putting on cloak.*] I can't spend the night in a strange man's house.

HELMER But can we not live here, as brother and sister...?